Resilience coaching
tool kit

Practical self-management exercises for professionals working to enhance the well-being of clients.

CPD
CERTIFIED
The CPD Certification
Service

Laurel Alexander

Pavilion

The Resilience Coaching Toolkit

A resource manual for professionals working with people to increase awareness of resilience and self-management approaches

© Laurel Alexander

The author has asserted her rights in accordance with the Copyright, Designs and Patents Act 1988 to be identified as the author of this work.

Published by:
Pavilion Publishing and Media Ltd
Rayford House
School Road
Hove BN3 5HX
UK

Tel: 01273 434 943
Fax: 01273 227 308

Published 2017

A catalogue record for this book is available from the British Library

ISBN: 978-1-911028-39-0

Pavilion is the leading training and development provider and publisher in the health, social care and allied fields, providing a range of innovative training solutions underpinned by sound research and professional values. We aim to put our customers first, through excellent customer service and value.

Author: Laurel Alexander
Editor: Mike Benge, Pavilion Publishing and Media
Cover design: Emma Dawe, Pavilion Publishing and Media
Page layout and typesetting: Emma Dawe, Pavilion Publishing and Media
Printing: CMP Digital Print Solutions

Contents

Introduction

About this pack

Welcome to the *Resilience Coaching Toolkit*. This pack has been created to introduce you to the principles of resilience coaching and to enable you to deliver training and guidance to increase people's awareness of resilience and self-management approaches. It is designed to help coaches and trainers deliver coaching to individuals as well as groups, and to enable the creation of flexible learning programmes that can be customised to cater for an individual client's or group's needs.

The resource will assist learners to:

▶ understand the basic principles of resilience

▶ explore what resilience means to them

▶ practice techniques that can be used in daily life.

Who can use this resource and with whom?

This resource is designed for health and social care professionals to use with different user groups. Here are some examples:

▶ Counsellors and psychotherapists coaching clients who have mild depression.

▶ Mental health support workers delivering community services incorporating coaching into small group and one-to-one work.

▶ A school business manager using resilience coaching with staff to ease the passage of internal change.

▶ Nurses coaching young diabetics (18–25) on a one-to-one basis and in small groups, in person and over Skype.

▶ Nurses working with COPD (chronic obstructive pulmonary disease) and heart failure patients delivering one-to-one wellness coaching in person or within the patient's home.

▶ A wellness coach working in a health and well-being centre run jointly by Turning Point and the NHS in-centre in London, delivering coaching to members of the public with mild mental health problems.

▶ Internal staff working in the corporate sector delivering resilience coaching to employees.

▶ Personal trainers using resilience coaching to motivate clients.

▶ A career development specialist using resilience coaching as part of a redundancy package with clients.

- ▶ Youth workers using health and well-being coaching with young people.
- ▶ Volunteer workers using resilience coaching with clients who have low level mental health issues.
- ▶ A social worker and community tutor working in partnership delivering health and well-being coaching to groups of women in a family centre.
- ▶ A business coach delivering entrepreneurial resilience workshops to business start-ups.
- ▶ A wellness coach/therapist delivering one-to-one resilience coaching to women going through the breast cancer journey.
- ▶ A trainer/coach tutor delivering group resilience coaching to front line workers from MIND.

Links to coaching qualifications

Laurel Alexander, author of this resource and Director of Studies for Wellness Professionals at Work, offers the following accredited coaching qualifications:

- ▶ Diploma in Resilience Coaching (accredited with National Council of Psychotherapists)
- ▶ Diploma in Life Coaching Skills (accredited with Association for Coaching and National Council of Psychotherapists)
- ▶ Diploma in Wellness Coaching (accredited with Association for Coaching and National Council of Psychotherapists)
- ▶ Integrated Diploma in Resilience and Wellness Coaching (accredited with National Council of Psychotherapists)

Most of the skills covered in this resource are included in the above diplomas.

Train the Resilience Coach Certificate

Wellness Professionals at Work (WP@W) is proud to offer the Train the Resilience Coach Certificate, based on the Resilience Coaching Toolkit, which carries CPD points from the CPD Certification Service. The Certificate offers additional accreditation as WP@W is an accredited CPD Centre with the National Council of Psychotherapists.

Defining resilience

Psychological resilience might be defined as an individual's ability to successfully absorb negative life events, to adapt and to continue tackling life tasks in the face of adverse conditions. Resilient people don't dwell on failures – instead they acknowledge their situation, learn from their mistakes, and they move on. This doesn't mean 'being tough'; you can be resilient and still show emotions such as anger or sadness when things go wrong, but it means not being unduly affected by these emotions, or being able to move past the negative and get on with things, remaining positive:

'Resilience is the process of adapting well in the face of adversity, trauma, tragedy, threats or significant sources of stress – such as family and relationship problems, serious health problems or workplace and financial stressors. It means "bouncing back" from difficult experiences. Resilience is not a trait that people either have or do not have. It involves behaviors, thoughts and actions that can be learned and developed in anyone.' [1]

Key characteristics of resilience

Resilience involves a range of behaviours, thoughts and actions, all of which can be learned and developed. Factors which contribute to resilience include:

▶ **Developing mindful awareness:** Mindfulness, as a psychological concept, is the focusing of one's attention and awareness based on the concept within Buddhist meditation and popularised in the West by Jon Kabat-Zinn[2]. Practising mindfulness can help people begin to recognise their habitual patterns of mind, allowing them to respond in new ways and so build resilience.

▶ **Taking ownership:** Personal responsibility is the belief that successes or failures are determined by your own talents and motivations as opposed to external forces such as luck or good timing. Those who take ownership believe they control their own destiny and attribute events to their own traits. Rather than relying on external factors such as luck to achieve objectives, they look inward to their own talents and motivations and attempt to exert control over situations.

▶ **Understanding personal values:** Who we are is what we become and do. If we are to be authentic, our personal values need to underpin our choices and actions.

▶ **Managing strong emotions:** We are a mixture of thoughts and feelings and sometimes one is stronger than the other. For example, we may hide our emotions behind a rational persona or we may become over-emotional at the expense of rationality. Resilience is a balance between these two states.

▶ **Effective questioning:** Effective questioning enables us to become informed so that we are better placed to make decisions and take action.

▶ **Active listening:** We have one mouth and two ears, suggesting that we need to listen more than we talk. Active listening is crucial to resilience. If we don't understand something or we are in conflict with another, we need to engage with effective questioning and active listening in order to inform and measure our response.

▶ **Building perseverance:** Grit, tenacity, endurance, persistence – these are the essence of resilience. It's not about a lack of problems. It's not about always feeling happy, confident and positive. Perseverance is having the spirit to keep moving forward.

▶ **Developing a non-judgemental mindset:** We're all full of judgement. Even as you read this, you're making a judgement of yourself as to whether you're judgemental!

---

1 APA (2016) *The Road to Resilience* [online]. Available at: http://www.apa.org/helpcenter/road-resilience.aspx (accessed December 2016).
2 Kabat-Zinn J (1994) *Wherever You Go, There You Are*. Hyperion: New York.

We judge ourselves and others, which often results in internal and external conflict. Resilience is the absence (or reduction) of a non-judgemental mindset.

▶ **Developing problem-solving skills:** Most of us tend to focus on problems, wasting time on the whys and wherefores; on weakness and failures. The resilient person focuses on solutions.

▶ **Improving confidence and self-esteem:** Confidence is the outer shell to self-esteem. We can appear confident outside but have low self-esteem on the inside. A resilient person is someone who experiences high self-esteem but on bad days knows how to support themselves with self-compassion.

▶ **Assertive communication:** Assertiveness and self-esteem go hand in hand. When we feel good about ourselves, we show our resilience through assertiveness.

▶ **Fostering self-care:** Self-care comes in both psychological and physical forms. For example, by taking mental time-out, through having a healthy diet and taking appropriate exercise. Taking care of yourself helps to keep your mind and body primed to deal with situations that require resilience.

▶ **Improving self-compassion:** A resilient person is kind to themselves. They know that everyone has foibles and failings, occasionally falling but always getting back up and moving forward.

▶ **Changing perspective:** Sometimes our mindset becomes fixed and we can't see the wood for the trees. A resilient person is able to move their mind, tries to see things from different perspectives and so finds fresh vision and new approaches to problems.

▶ **Improving adaptability:** Challenges occur on a daily basis, and when life presents you with one that is insurmountable, resilient people accept the circumstances that cannot be changed while focusing on circumstances that they can influence. A more adaptable mindset allows us to evaluate and adjust to the different challenges we have each day.

▶ **Viewing change as opportunity:** Things change from second to second. Rather than being resistant to, or fearful of, change, resilient people embrace change and see it as an opportunity.

▶ **Increasing pro-activity:** Taking decisive action rather than detaching from adverse situations is a trait of the resilient person. Although it can take time to recover from a set-back, knowing that your situation can improve if you work at it can help. Resilient people pro-actively work on solving a problem rather than letting themselves get paralysed by negativity.

▶ **Personal networking:** Good relationships with family members, friends and others strengthen resilience.

▶ **Increasing optimism:** Resilient people possess an ability to experience both negative and positive emotions, even in difficult situations. Our brains are wired to pay more attention to negative events than positive ones. However, in reality we experience positive events more often. One key to building resilience lies in noticing and appreciating those positive experiences with more frequency.

▶ **Increasing empathy:** Empathy is an ability that contributes to resilience by helping us appreciate other points of view, which can then help us to get our problems into perspective.

▶ **Laughter and humour:** Humour is a subjective matter and what one person finds funny will not necessarily be shared by another person. Laughter can make the unbearable bearable and so builds resilience. As psychiatrist Victor Frankl wrote in *Man's Search for Meaning*[3] about surviving Nazi concentration camps: '*Humor was another of the soul's weapons in the fight for self-preservation. It is well known that humor, more than anything else in the human makeup, can afford aloofness and an ability to rise above any situation, even if only for a few seconds.*'

▶ **Extending purpose and meaning:** When life has meaning, we have a stronger sense of purpose and this helps develop resilience.

Areas of resilience

When we begin to first look at resilience, we tend to think of relaxing ourselves physically or trying to ease anxiety in relation to a particular situation. However, our sense of resilience doesn't build in isolation of the rest of our life. It is also influenced by life factors such as our social interactions, environmental influences, work practices and values/beliefs. In other words, there are a number of different life areas in which to build resilience:

Psychological resilience: Just as our bodies need to be exercised and stretched, so do our minds. Mental activities such as learning, problem-solving and creating help to build cognitive resilience.

Emotional resilience: To be emotionally resilient is to be aware of our emotional nature and to find ways of appropriately communicating and working with it. It entails taking responsibility to tackle our emotional challenges with intelligence, and ensure we behave appropriately in our relationships with others. Emotional well-being involves fulfilling our emotional needs by enhancing our self-esteem and appropriate mental health care.

Physical resilience: As we all know, optimum physical fitness can be achieved by following a healthy lifestyle – getting regular exercise, eating a healthy diet, abstaining from harmful habits such as drug and alcohol abuse, and protecting ourselves from injury. When we feel physically well, we enjoy a more positive frame of mind and better self-esteem. In addition, part of our physical resilience is medical well-being, which involves the appropriate use of conventional and complementary medical systems.

Social resilience: In his book *Love and Survival*[4], Dean Ornish reviewed the scientific literature and found that adults who related well with their parents, people who have an integrated community of friendships, and males who feel loved by their partner have lower rates of disease and death. These findings led Ornish to speculate that social factors may be as important as physical factors in determining overall health.

3 Frankl V (1959) *Man's Search for Meaning*. London: Rider Books.
4 Ornish D (1998) *Love and Survival*. New York: Harper Collins.

Social resilience comes from a sense of family and friendship as well as local and global community. It involves positive interactions with others and the development of close friendships and intimacy. Social resilience is built on communication skills, the caring for others and allowing others to care for you.

Spiritual resilience: Spiritual resilience can be built upon guiding beliefs or values that provide life direction. The National Wellbeing Institute describes spiritual well-being as follows: '*It is better to ponder the meaning of life for ourselves and to be tolerant of the beliefs of others than to close our minds and become intolerant. It is better to live each day in a way that is consistent with our values and beliefs than to do otherwise and feel untrue to ourselves.*'[5] When we achieve spiritual well-being, we integrate our inner values and beliefs with our external actions. As Socrates said, '*The unexamined life is not worth living*'. When someone's spiritual resilience is strong, they have a strong sense of purpose in their existence and strength in times of crisis.

Occupational resilience: An occupation includes paid jobs or a career, or unpaid work such as voluntary or community work. Occupational resilience can give your life meaning and involves choosing work or activities that are consistent with your values, interests and beliefs. Achieving optimal occupational resilience allows you to maintain a positive attitude in order to use your skills and pursue your goals.

The resilience coaching model

The resilience coaching model is a non-directive approach whereby the facilitator encourages the learner to self-manage their own resilience pro-actively.

Passive resilience coaching	Pro-active resilience coaching
Focused on short-term results	Focus on long-term behaviour change
Focused on deficits	Strength focused
Based on instruction	Based on asking questions
One size fits all	Personalised
Medically focused	Whole-person focused
Problem-oriented	Solution-oriented

Using the pro-active approach you can help the learner:

▶ make a conscious decision to shape a more resilient lifestyle

▶ assume responsibility for the quality of their life

▶ understand that resilience is the integration of mind, body and spirit

▶ make changes to enhance their resilience

▶ learn the difference between what they can change and what they cannot, and to help them focus their energies wisely

▶ develop a resilient lifestyle that will allow them to revitalise and re-energise themselves so that they can continue to thrive in the face of the ongoing external demands of life

---

5 UCR (2017) *Spiritual Wellness* [online]. Available at: https://wellness.ucr.edu/spiritual_wellness.html (accessed March 2017).

- prepare to cope with change

- learn how to control their thoughts and emotions

- find a conscious balance between activity and rest

- create a sense of connection and meaning in their life.

Taking a non-directive approach means that the learner keeps control over the content and pace of the resilience development process, which then becomes about whatever the learner wants to get from it. A fundamental principle of being learner-centered is that they can find their own answers and therefore move towards resilience in their own way. As a trainer or coach, this is facilitated by you through:

- listening to how things are from the learner's point of view

- checking your understanding with the learner

- treating the learner with respect and regard

- being self-aware and self-accepting (you know yourself and are willing to be known by the learner).

As a facilitator using coaching skills, you accompany the learner on their journey by using your knowledge and expertise to understand them as fully as possible. It is by reflecting back that understanding that the learner becomes more self-aware and finds their own process of developing resilience. Your role is one of experienced facilitator, helping learners to clarify and connect with their natural intuition about what feels right, and offering them a space to discover a path that will take them towards their goals.

Working in partnership

A standard coaching principle is that the facilitator/coach and learner work together in a partnership of equals[6]. In coaching for resilience we need to think about the power dynamics that may affect the relationship and that may be more apparent than in non-clinical coaching situations.

Your role is to travel with the learner on their journey (not yours), and to facilitate the creative process in ways that are right for that individual. It is important that the learner does not foster dependence on you. It is equally crucial that you don't present an aura of infallibility or that you have all the answers. Here are some of the skills you will need:

- Active listening.

- Being non-judgemental/non-paternalistic.

- Having an ability to support people, combined with challenging them at a level that is individually appropriate.

- Effective questioning.

- Summarising.

- Reflecting.

---

6 Rogers J (2008) *Coaching Skills: A handbook* (2nd ed). Maidenhead: McGraw Hill Open University Press.

▶ Giving feedback.

▶ Allowing space.

▶ Using clinical expertise (if qualified) to inform.

▶ Encouraging the learner's resourcefulness.

▶ Allowing the learner to set the agenda.

Using the resilience coaching toolkit

Each of the activities in this training resource has a short introduction to the subject area, followed by a brief delivery outline with approximate timings, suggested handouts and PowerPoint slides. All of the activities are suitable for group work, while some can also be adapted easily for one-to-one work.

1:1 work

When working one to one with a client, choose activities according to the learner's needs. You may need to demonstrate a skill or behaviour in order for the learner to gain the most from the activity. Make sure the learner's understand why they're doing the activity, how it is relevant to them and that they know what to do. Watch how they engage with it. Provide constructive feedback and encourage discussion following the activity, for example, ask them what the activity was like to do, how they feel, what thoughts they have, what was challenging and what was easy.

 **Note:** not every activity is suitable for working on a one-to-one basis – those that are will be marked with the one-to-one symbol.

Group work

Introduce the activity in a whole group setting before engaging the learners in the process. Allow the activity to unfold while keeping an eye on development. At the end of the activity, bring the group back together and discuss experiences and outcomes. **Note:** all activities are suitable for groups.

Cut and pasting activities

You can use the activities in this resource in a variety of ways in order to make a short or long workshop for groups or individuals. You might divide workshop content over several separate sessions. Here are some workshop ideas which you can use as flexibly as your creativity allows:

Workshop title/ objective	Suggested activities
Building confidence	Developing mindful awareness - Taking ownership - Understanding personal values - Managing strong emotions - Active listening - Effective questioning - Building perseverance - Developing problem-solving skills - Assertive communication - Improving confidence and self-esteem - Fostering self-care - Improving self-compassion - Changing perspective - Improving adaptability - Viewing change as opportunity - Increasing pro-activity - Increasing optimism - Laughter and humour - Extending purpose and meaning
Improving assertiveness	Developing Mindful Awareness - Taking ownership - Understanding Personal Values - Managing Strong Emotions - Active Listening - Effective Questioning - Building Perseverance - Developing a Non-Judgemental Mindset - Developing Problem-solving Skills - Assertive Communication - Advancing Confidence and Self-Esteem - Changing Perspective - Improving Adaptability - Increasing Pro-Activity - Personal Networking - Increasing Empathy
Managing change	Developing mindful awareness - Taking ownership - Managing strong emotions - Active listening - Effective questioning - Building perseverance - Developing a non-judgemental mindset - Developing problem-solving skills - Assertive communication - Advancing confidence and self-esteem - Fostering self-care - Changing perspective - Improving adaptability - Viewing change as opportunity - Increasing pro-activity - Personal networking – Laughter and humour - Increasing optimism
Increasing self-care	Developing mindful awareness - Taking ownership - Managing strong emotions - Developing problem-solving skills - Assertive communication - Advancing confidence and self-esteem - Fostering self-care - Improving self-compassion - Extending purpose and meaning
Time management	Developing mindful awareness - Taking ownership - Developing problem-solving skills - Assertive communication - Fostering self-Care - Changing perspective - Improving adaptability - Viewing change as opportunity - Increasing pro-activity - Personal networking
Personal development	Developing mindful awareness - Taking ownership - Understanding personal values - Managing strong emotions - Active listening - Effective questioning - Building perseverance - Developing a non-judgemental mindset - Developing problem-solving skills - Assertive communication - Improving confidence and self-esteem - Fostering self-care - Improving self-compassion - Changing perspective - Improving adaptability - Viewing change as opportunity - Increasing pro-activity - Personal networking - Increasing optimism - Increasing empathy - Extending purpose and meaning

Workshop title/ objective	Suggested activities
Goal setting	Developing mindful awareness - Taking ownership - Understanding personal values - Building perseverance - Developing problem-solving skills - Improving confidence and self-esteem - Changing perspective - Improving adaptability - Viewing change as opportunity - Increasing pro-activity - Personal networking
Presenting a positive image	Developing mindful awareness - Taking ownership - Understanding personal values - Managing strong emotions - Active listening - Effective questioning - Developing a non-judgemental mindset - Assertive communication - Improving confidence and self-esteem - Improving self-compassion - Changing perspective - Improving adaptability - Personal networking - Increasing optimism - Laugher and humour - Increasing empathy
Building better relationships	Developing mindful awareness - Taking ownership - Managing strong emotions - Active listening - Effective questioning - Developing a non-judgemental mindset - Assertive communication - Improving confidence and self-esteem - Changing perspective - Improving adaptability - Increasing pro-activity - Personal networking – Laughter and humour - Increasing empathy

For group work, consider the group size, participant engagement abilities and the desired outcomes before choosing the relevant activities.

For individual work, consider the individual's engagement abilities and the desired outcome before choosing an activity. You might choose to take one activity and divide the delivery over two or more sessions.

Between session activities

Based on the activities, it is a good idea for learners to make guided journal reflections. This may be a written exercise and/or an agreed between-session activity that they may also record in a journal.

CD-ROM/online resources

The CD-ROM includes learner handouts and optional PowerPoint slides to introduce each activity.

Symbol guide

 1:1 suitability

 Discussion points

 Handouts

 PowerPoint Slides

Suggested reading around resilience

If you would like to know more about resilience, here are some suggested titles that might help you.

▶ *Developing Resilience* by Michael Neenan

▶ *Positivity* by Dr Barbara Fredrickson

▶ *Change Your Questions, Change Your Life* by Marilee Adams

▶ *The Coaching Manual* by Julie Starr

▶ *Brilliant Emotional Intelligence* by Gill Hasson

▶ *Time to Write to Yourself: A guide to journaling for emotional health and self-development* by Dianne Sandland

▶ *Relaxation and Stress Reduction Workbook* by Martha Davis, Elizabeth Robbins Eshelman and Matthew McKay

▶ *Develop Your Assertiveness (Creating Success)* by Sue Bishop

▶ *Self-Esteem: A proven program of cognitive techniques for assessing, improving and maintaining your self-esteem* by Matthew McKay, Patrick Fanning

▶ *Overcoming Anxiety: A self-help guide using CBT* by Helen Kennerley

▶ *Overcoming Anger and Irritability: A self-help guide using CBT* by William Davies

▶ *Emotional Intelligence & Working with Emotional Intelligence* by Daniel Goleman

▶ *The Little CBT Workbook* by Dr Michael Sinclair and Dr Belinda Hollingsworth

▶ *Wherever You Go, There You Are: Mindfulness meditation for everyday life* by Jon Kabat Zinn

▶ *Solution Focused Coaching in Practice (Essential Coaching Skills and Knowledge)* by Bill O'Connell, Stephen Palmer and Helen Williams

Unit 1: Developing mindful awareness

Introduction

Jon Kabat-Zinn describes mindfulness as an approach to life based on the understanding that 'the present is the only time that any of us have to be alive – to know anything – to perceive – to learn – to act – to change – to heal'[7].

Mindfulness practice is the ability to pay deliberate attention to our internal and external experiences from moment to moment in a non-judgmental, open and curious way. Within the practice of mindfulness, thoughts and feelings are observed as events in the mind, without over-analysing them and reacting to them in habitual patterns. This self-observation introduces a space between our perceptions and responses. Mindfulness can help loosen the rigidity of our faulty mindsets, opening us up to more creative and productive ways of thinking, which in turn improves our resilience.

Depending on group size, it will take about 2hrs 25 mins to work through all of the activities in this unit.

Aims

This unit aims to teach learners about mindful awareness and how to develop it. By the end of the session they should be able to experience mindfulness through:

▶ body scanning

▶ their senses

▶ micro-mindfulness

▶ listening

▶ breathing

▶ contemplation.

---

7 Kabat-Zinn J (1990) *Full Catastrophe Living.* Random House.

Activities

Body scan

 1-2-1

Time: 30 minutes

Resources:

 Handout 1.1: Body Scan

 PowerPoint Slide 2: Developing mindfulness

Instructions:

Reading the introduction to this unit to the group, or using your own knowledge, explain about mindfulness practice.

Show **PowerPoint Slide 2: Developing mindfulness** and introduce the concept and importance of body sensation awareness in relation to mindfulness. Explain that we all spend much time in our thoughts and feelings and can easily become focused on the past or future. Developing mindfulness through body sensation awareness enables us to bring our mind down into our body and so into the present moment.

Next, give out copies of **Handout 1.1** and take learners through the body awareness exercise.

Finally, bring everyone back into a larger group to debrief, using the discussion points below if needed.

 Discussion points: What was it like doing the activity? What did the learner/s discover about themselves?

Micro-mindfulness

 1-2-1

Time: 15 minutes

Resources:

 Handout 1.2: Ways to be mindful

Instructions:

Refer the group to the last paragraph in **Handout 1.2** and introduce the subject of applying mindfulness to a particular task and how this might be done. Explain that, as the handout says, whatever you're doing, to apply mindfulness to a task you need to focus totally on the task in hand. You first need to view it as a positive event and an exercise in self-understanding, rather than simply as a task. Truly focus on all the aspects and use all your senses. You can apply mindfulness to domestic tasks, work, personal care and your hobby or community activities.

Ask the learner/s to make a hot or cold drink while being totally present in the activity. Debrief by discussing the exercise using the points below if needed. Extend the activity to drinking the drink before discussing, if there you have time.

Finally, ask the learners to read through **Handout 1.2** after the session as a short piece of homework.

 Discussion points: What was it like doing the activity? What did they discover about themselves?

Mindful listening

 1-2-1

Time: 15 minutes

Instructions:

Introduce the concept of mindful listening. Ask the learners to listen mindfully for five minutes.

Listening is one of the five vital senses which we tend to take for granted. We can mindfully listen to someone on different levels:

▶ Notwithstanding a physical issue, we can all *hear*. However, *listening* goes beyond hearing. Hearing is a sound, a noise, while listening takes more effort to discern what one hears e.g. a voice speaking or crying, a tone of voice, the words said or not said.

▶ Active listening is a more mindful activity. In order to do active listening, we need to be present in the moment to hear the words, tone and pace of the person speaking and to hear in more depth what they are saying, and what they're not.

Mindful listening in the sense of this activity is taking the time to stop with eyes open or closed, and really pay attention to every sound you can hear, whether it is internal, inside your body, or external, such as inside the room or coming from outside. Mindful listening is noting and allowing the sound to pass without attachment.

 Discussion points: What was it like doing the activity? What did the learner/s discover about themselves?

Mindful breathing

 1-2-1

Time: 15 minutes

Instructions:

Breathing is a core involuntary activity that most of us do without thought. Explain that you can look at mindful breathing in two ways.

There are normally two ways of breathing, chest or abdominal. Chest breathing is shallow, irregular and fast. It can also activate the stress response and is therefore more connected to anxiety and shallow breathing. The other way of breathing is abdominal breathing. On inhaling, the lungs open fully to allow as much oxygen to enter the system as possible. Abdominal breathing slows you down. It is also efficient, bringing a good supply of oxygen to your brain. Check your breathing pattern by putting one hand on your chest and one hand on your stomach. If your lower hand moves and your top hand does not, you are doing abdominal breathing. But if your top hand moves and your bottom one does not, you are doing chest breathing.

Explain that you are now going to do an abdominal breathing activity.

Ask the learner/s to inhale through their noses and exhale out of their mouths. Their exhalation needs to be longer than their inhalation. To slow their exhalation down let their breath out as if they're blowing out a candle (purse their lips). Next, read out the following instructions and take the learner/s through these exercises:

▶ Lay down flat and place your hands fingertip to fingertip with your middle fingers meeting at your belly button.

▶ As you inhale through your nose, push your belly up and feel your fingertips expand. Rest a beat before exhaling slowly through your mouth. Rest a beat before inhaling again and feel your belly rise. Repeat this cycle five times.

▶ Now place your hands under the breast area of each side of your body, which is the rib area.

▶ As you inhale through your nose, expand your ribs and feel your hands push out. Rest a beat before exhaling slowly through your mouth. Rest a beat before inhaling again and feel your ribs expand. Repeat this cycle five times.

▶ Now you are going to do a complete breathing cycle, inhaling deeply from the belly and ribcage and exhaling completely.

▶ As you inhale through your nose for a count of five, push your belly up and expand your ribs. Rest a beat, before exhaling slowly through your mouth for a count of six. Rest a beat before inhaling again and feel your belly rise and your ribs expand. Repeat this cycle five times.

Next, explain you're going to do a mindful activity. Read the following instructions and take the learner/s through the activity:

► Find a comfortable position either sitting or lying on your back. Close your eyes or soften your gaze.

► Focus your awareness on your environment and any sounds you might hear.

► Focus your awareness on your body and complete a body scan.

► Focus your awareness on your breathing. Notice the sensation of your breath going in and out of your nostrils or mouth. Observe how the air feels going in and out. Keep your mind focused on the breath going in and out of your nostrils or mouth.

► Now pay attention to the rise and fall of your chest as you breathe.

► Now notice the rise and fall of your belly.

► Now you're going to put your mindful breathing together. Follow the breath for its full duration, from the start to finish. Notice that the breath happens on its own, without any conscious effort. Some breaths may be slow, some fast, some shallow or deep. You don't need to control or change the breath, just notice it.

 Discussion points: What was it like doing the activity? What did the learner/s discover about themselves?

Five senses mindfulness log

 1-2-1

Time: 15 minutes

Resources:

 Handout 1.3: Mindfulness log

 PowerPoint Slide 2: Developing mindfulness

PowerPoint Slide 3: The five senses

Instructions:

Show **PowerPoint Slide 2: Developing mindfulness** and explain to the learners that the more frantic our lives get, the more important it is to take quick breaks throughout the day to calm down and clear our heads. Show **PowerPoint Slide 3: The five senses** and explain that focusing on the five senses can help shift our focus away from our worries. It can also help us develop an awareness of and gratitude for the world around us and the small everyday blessings we might otherwise take for granted.

Next, give out copies of **Handout 1.3: Mindfulness log**. You can either facilitate the learners in experiencing their five senses during the session and they can they complete the log before the end, or you could ask the learners to complete the plan over the coming week. Whatever works best for you, explain your instructions to the group.

Finally, gather everyone back into a group to discuss the activity, using the discussion points below if necessary.

 Discussion points: What was it like doing the activity? What did they discover about themselves?

Contemplation

 1-2-1

Time: 10 minutes

Resources:

 Handout 1.4: Contemplation

Instructions:

Give out **Handout 1.4: Contemplation** to each of the learners and ask them to contemplate and look at one of the images for at least two minutes. Tell them that if they become restless, they should shift their gaze to focus on a different part of the image, or scan slowly from one side of the image to the other, or to slowly move closer to and farther away from the image.

Debrief the group using the discussion points below if needed.

 Discussion points: What was it like doing the activity? What did they discover about themselves? Ask:

▶ What did you first notice about this image?

▶ What else did you notice as you kept looking at it?

▶ What thoughts went through your mind while you were looking at this image?

▶ What feelings or memories (if any) did it bring up for you?

Window frame

 1-2-1

Time: 15 minutes

Instructions:

Ask the learners to look out the nearest window as if it's a painting or photo of a landscape or a cityscape, and ask them to mindfully observe what they see for five minutes, as they did with the image in the last activity.

Debrief the group using the discussion points below if needed..

 Discussion points: What was it like doing the activity? What did they discover about themselves? Ask:

▶ What colours and patterns did you see?

▶ If you were a painter or photographer, how would you choose to represent this image?

▶ How does the image change when you move slightly forward and backward or take half a step to the right or left?

Journal reflections and post-session practice

Ask the learner/s to choose one mindful activity each day from the following list:

▶ Mindful listening.

▶ Check your posture or do a body scan.

▶ See, heal and feel: see three things, hear three things and feel three things.

▶ Micro-mindfulness: complete one small activity as mindfully as you can.

▶ Mindful breathing: spend five minutes breathing mindfully.

▶ Window frame: spend five minutes on this exercise.

▶ The mindful photo: selecting an image to photograph can also be a great way to stay in the moment and practice mindful seeing. Focus on small subjects. Mindful seeing is behaving as if you really haven't seen a particular object before. Observe your emotions e.g. wanting to get the next good shot. Sometimes, wanting to take a photo can get in the way of directly experiencing what is present.

They should also complete their five senses mindfulness log for one week before their next session.

Unit 2: Taking ownership

Introduction

Taking ownership means a person holds him or herself accountable for the outcomes that result from their choices, behaviours and actions. When someone accepts that their current situation is the result of the choices they have made, they understand that no one else is pulling the strings of their life unless they allow them to. A person can therefore make the decision to change, and this decision to take ownership will guide them towards a path of resilience.

Depending on group size, it will take about 2hrs 25mins to work through all of the activities in this unit.

Aims

This unit aims to teach learners about taking ownership and how to develop it. By the end of the session, they should be able to experience ownership through:

▶ problem solving

▶ peer coaching

▶ leading.

Activities

Problem solving

Time: 20 minutes

Instructions:

Explain the link between ownership and problem-solving. Problems arise for all of us from time to time, either external problems such as a change in job responsibilities, or a more internal problem with ourselves, such as needing to cut down on the amount of sugar we consume or increase the amount of exercise we get.

When faced with a problem, we can either be re-active and defensive or we can be pro-active and take ownership. While an externally presented problem, such as a job-role change, may not have been down to us, we still have a choice of how we respond and it's this choice that gives us ownership over our mindset, our choices, decisions and consequent behaviours in relation to problem-solving.

Ask the learners to work in pairs and each to identify a problem they are willing to share. Using listening and questioning skills, each assists the other in finding a possible solution. Then come back into the larger group to share what they discussed, using the points below if needed.

 Discussion points: What was it like doing the activity? What did they discover about themselves?

How to take ownership

 1-2-1

Time: 30 minutes

Resources:

 Handout 2.1: How to take ownership

Instructions:

Option 1: Ask the learners to work in pairs and to identify a problem to discuss with their partner.

The learner sharing their problem first identifies what constitutes a successful outcome to the problem. In pairs and with the partner supporting the person sharing, the learner charts their own solution to achieve that outcome. This allows the learner to build a relationship with their solution, thereby increasing their ownership of it. This means accepting that the responsibility for problem-solving is theirs, and involves developing a mindset that they are accountable for the quality and timeliness of a solution, even when they're working with others to solve a problem.

Option 2: Using **Handout 2.1: How to Take Ownership,** each learner could choose one point to in the handout discuss in small groups. Then gather back into the larger group to discuss.

 Discussion points: What was it like doing the activity? What did they discover about themselves?

Workplace ownership

 1-2-1

Time: 15 minutes

Instructions:

Ownership at work is about being a problem-solver. Taking ownership means you hold yourself accountable for your actions and how you complete your work. Whatever your role, taking ownership is about backing up your actions with commitment.

Introduce the subject of taking ownership in the workplace, which can happen in different ways such as being involved in goal setting and action-planning, timekeeping, career development, prioritising workload, communicating with colleagues and self-care e.g. life/work balance.

Use the discussion points below to explore the issues further.

 Discussion points:

▶ What benefit do learners think they could get out of being allowed to take more ownership in the workplace, the benefits to their boss, the organisation and the customer?

▶ What are the problems of them taking ownership, for them, their boss, the organisation and the customer?

▶ What areas of their work would they like to be encouraged to take ownership of?

▶ What support do they need from their boss in order to take ownership?

Exploring ownership

 1-2-1

Time: 30 minutes

Resources:

 Handout 2.2: Consequences of not taking ownership

Handout 2.3: Benefits of taking ownership

 PowerPoint Slide 4: Low-ownership

PowerPoint Slide 5: High-ownership

PowerPoint Slide 6: Freedom

Instructions:

Give out copies of **Handout 2.2: Consequences of not taking ownership**. Give them some time to read through it and then ask them to get into small groups to discuss how they (or others) might avoid taking ownership. Then gather everyone back into the larger group to discuss.

Repeat the process using **Handout 2.3: Benefits of taking ownership**.

Next, ask the learners to identify what low ownership looks like before showing **PowerPoint Slide 4: Low ownership**.

Ask the learners to identify what high ownership looks like before using **PowerPoint Slide 5: High ownership**.

Show **PowerPoint Slide 6: Freedom and ownership** and open a discussion on who can influence our ownership mindset e.g. parents, teachers etc.

 Discussion points: What does taking ownership like look like for the learner/s on a day-to-day basis?

Peer coaching

Time: 20 minutes

Instructions:

Peer coaching is a way to improve a learner's critical thinking skills and ownership. Put the group into groups of three. Each member of the group then takes turns to be 'coach', 'coachee' and 'observer'. Ask the coach to demonstrate to the coachee a simple activity they feel confident with e.g. a dance step, an exercise movement, a meditation, a deep breathing technique, saying a tongue twister etc… anything the coachee can copy. Upon completion, the observer provides feedback to the coach on what they could have done better and where they were successful. Gather everyone back into a larger group to debrief.

 Discussion points: What was it like doing the activity? What did they discover about themselves?

Lead

Time: 1 hour

Instructions:

Another great way to foster a sense of ownership is to have each learner lead an activity such as a simple exercise, a dance routine or how to make a paper plane. This could be done as a whole group or divide the group in smaller groups of four.

Gather everyone back into larger group to debrief using the points below if needed.

 Discussion points: What was it like doing the activity? What did they discover about themselves?

Journal reflections and post-session practice

Ask the participant/s to observe themselves in action and be mindful of when they take ownership of something and when they don't. Review this journal at the next session.

Unit 3: Understanding personal values

Introduction

Values are important principles that you hold in high regard and guide the way you live your life and the decisions you make. They determine your priorities, and are the measures you use to see that your life is turning out the way you want. A value is formed by a particular belief that is related to the worth of an idea or behaviour and can influence many of the judgments you make.

The beliefs that we hold, be they religious, cultural or moral, are an important part of our identity and they come from our real experiences. However, we often forget that the original experience that gave rise to a belief is not the same as what is happening in life now. For example, negative conflict with our mothers early in life can create a belief that all women in authority are 'out to get us'. A combination of a person's values and beliefs affect the quality of their current experience. The example above could lead to having issues with women in authority in the workplace.

When the things that you do and the way you behave match your values, your resilience increases and you feel satisfied. But when these don't align, that's when things feel wrong.

Depending on group size, it will take about 1hr 30mins to work through all of the activities in this unit.

Aims

This unit aims to teach learners about understanding personal values. By the end of the session, they should be able to identify and prioritise some of their more important values.

Activities

Identifying values: feeling happy

 1-2-1

Time: 15 minutes

Instructions:

Working in small groups, ask the learner/s to identify a time in their personal and professional lives when they felt particularly happy and they were making positive choices. You could ask questions such as:

▶ Think back to a recent event in your personal life where you made a choice which made you feel happy. What happened? In this situation, what worked well?

▶ Think back to a recent event in your professional life where you made a choice which made you feel happy. What happened? In this situation, what worked well?

Coming back in to the larger group, hold a general discussion using the points below if needed.

 Discussion points: What was it like doing the activity? What did the learner/s discover about themselves?

What were they doing? Were they with other people? If so, who? What other factors contributed to their happiness?

Identifying values: feeling proud

 1-2-1

Time: 15 minutes

Instructions:

Working in small groups, ask the learner/s to identify a time in their personal and professional life when they felt especially proud they were making positive choices. You could ask questions such as:

▶ Think back to a recent event in your personal life where you made a choice which made you feel proud. What happened? In this situation what worked well?

▶ Think back to a recent event in your professional life where you made a choice which made you feel proud. What happened? In this situation what worked well?

Coming back in to the larger group, you could use the discussion points set out below.

 Discussion points: What was it like doing the activity? What did they discover about themselves? Why were they proud? Did other people share their pride? If so, who? What other factors contributed to their feelings of pride?

Identifying values: feeling fulfilled

 1-2-1

Time: 15 minutes

Instructions:

Working in small groups, ask the learners to identify examples from their personal and professional life when they felt fulfilled they were making positive choices. You could ask questions such as:

▶ Think back to a recent event in your personal life where you made a choice which made you feel fulfilled. What happened? In this situation what worked well?

▶ Think back to a recent event in your professional life where you made a choice which made you feel fulfilled. What happened? In this situation what worked well?

Coming back in to the larger group, you could use the discussion point set out below.

 Discussion points: What was it like doing the activity? What did they discover about themselves?

What need or desire was fulfilled? How and why did the experience give their life meaning? What other factors contributed to their feelings of fulfilment?

Prioritising values

 1-2-1

Time: 15 minutes

Resources:

 Handout 3.1: Top values

Instructions:

Explain the following points to the learners:

▶ Values are important principles you hold in high regard and which guide the way you live your life and the decisions you make.

▶ They determine your priorities.

▶ A value is related to the worth of an idea or behaviour and can influence many of the judgments you make.

▶ What you believe are important qualities, or what qualities you admire in yourself and others, generally reflect your life experiences and the values which you established in your formative years through the influence of family, teachers, friends, religion, culture and education.

Next, give out **Handout 3.1: Top values** and ask the learner/s to:

▶ identify their own top 12 values from the list.

▶ write them down on a separate sheet of paper in no particular order.

▶ go down the list of values asking themselves which they would choose if they could satisfy only one of these values. This should identify their top value.

▶ ask the learners how their top values fit in with their life and vision.

Gather everyone into a big group and discuss the exercise using the points below.

 Discussion points: What was it like doing the activity? What did they discover about themselves?

Reaffirming your values

 1-2-1

Time: 15 minutes

Instructions:

Using their top priority personal values from the previous activity, start a general discussion with the leaner/s using the following questions:

▶ Do your top-priority personal values fit in with your life and vision for yourself?

▶ How do these values make you feel about yourself?

▶ How might you feel about telling your values to people you respect and admire?

▶ Do these values represent things you would support even if your choice isn't popular and puts you in the minority?

 Discussion points: What was it like doing the activity? What did they discover about themselves?

Where do values come from?

 1-2-1

Time: 15 minutes

Resources:

PowerPoint slide 7: Where do values come from?

PowerPoint Slide 8: Personal values

PowerPoint Slide 9: Values and beliefs

Instructions:

▶ Ask the learners where they think values come from before showing **PowerPoint Slide 7: Where do values come from?** to add to the discussion.

▶ Ask the learners how we can use our values before showing **PowerPoint Slide 8: Personal values**.

▶ Show **PowerPoint Slide 9: Values and beliefs** and hold a group discussion around the following points:

  ▶ Introduce how beliefs created in our past can underpin the choices we make now. Ask the learners to consider a current belief about relationships they may have now which has its roots in their past e.g. a belief learnt from their parents. Ask them to consider to what extent they still adhere to that belief and ask them to consider how that belief affects their current or recent relationships.

  ▶ Ask the learners to consider how beliefs contribute to our sense of religious, cultural or moral identity.

 Discussion points: What was it like doing the activity? What did they discover about themselves?

Journal reflections and post-session practice

Consider how your values show themselves in your life. For example, in your work, relationships or community activities. Record your thoughts on this in your journal over the coming days.

Unit 4: Managing strong emotions

Introduction

While we can have some control over our thought processes, our emotions can seem to have a life of their own. While it is relatively easy to stay with good emotions, it can be difficult to sit with strong emotions that are distressing. In an effort to avoid 'feeling bad' we may tend to either rationalise our emotions or repress them so that we not only avoid feeling bad, but we also avoid feeling good – in fact we can become almost emotionally numb.

A resilient person doesn't ignore or deny their strong feelings, they accept emotions and work with self-compassion to manage them.

Depending on group size, it will take about 5hrs 30mins to work through all of the activities in this unit.

Aims

This unit aims to teach learners about managing and working with strong emotions. By the end of the session, they should be able to:

▶ identify strong emotions in themselves and their body

▶ have a basic understanding of the link between thoughts, feelings and behaviours

▶ use the 'Stop, Drop and Process' technique

▶ understand the role of trust in being able to express strong emotions.

Activities

Identifying emotions

 1-2-1

Time: 30 minutes

Resources:

 Handout 4.1: Emotion word list

Instructions:

In this session you will be exploring with your learners how to identify different emotions. Explain that being able to accurately identify and put a name to an emotion they might be feeling is the first step to being able to manage that emotion. Give everyone a copy of **Handout 4.1: Emotion word list** and ask them to complete it.

 Discussion points: What was it like to complete the activity? What were your findings? Which emotions in general do you find difficult to deal with?

Emotional signals

 1-2-1

Time: 30 minutes

Resources:

 Handout 4.2: Identifying your emotional signals

Instructions:

Explain that you're next going to do an exercise to help your learners spot the signals that identify their emotions.

Give each learner a copy of **Handout 4.2: Identifying your emotional signals** and ask them to complete the first column listing their internal signals. Then, as a group or in one-to-one discussion, explore some of the responses that people recorded if they are willing to share them. Use the discussion points below to help aid the conversation if needed.

 Discussion points: What was it like doing the activity? What did you discover about yourself? Which questions were particularly helpful?

Strong emotions

 1-2-1

Time: 30 minutes

Resources:

 Handout 4.3: Managing strong emotions

 PowerPoint Slide 10: Methods for managing emotions

Instructions:

Explain that in this session you are going to be exploring different methods of managing strong emotions. To get them thinking, ask the group to offer suggestions as to how they currently manage their emotions, or how other people might.

Next, ask the learners to get into small groups, show **PowerPoint Slide 10** and give out copies of **Handout 4.3: Managing strong emotions**. Ask them to discuss different techniques and to use the handout as a guide. Then gather everyone back into a larger group to discuss further, using the points below if needed.

 Discussion points: What was it like to do the activity? What did you find out about yourself? What in particular do you find difficult? What is it like discussing your emotional well-being?

ABC

 1-2-1

Time: 30 minutes

Resources:

 Handout 4.5: Thought, emotion and behaviour

Handout 4.7: Negative thought patterns

Instructions:

Cognitive behaviour therapy (CBT) evolved out of Joseph Wolpe's behaviour therapy of the 1950s, which gradually combined with elements of Aaron Beck's cognitive therapy

(CT), Albert Ellis' rational-emotive behaviour therapy (REBT), and a number of other influences from the cognitive approaches to psychotherapy.

Cognitive behavioural approaches work on the principle that how we react to events is determined by our views of them, not by the events themselves. Through re-evaluating unhelpful mindsets (cognitive processes), we can implement alternative viewpoints that may be more effective in aiding problem-solving and changing behavior.

Albert Ellis developed the ABC model which describes the sequence of events that lead to the feelings we experience. He recommends that people break down their experience into these three areas in order to discover if irrational beliefs are present:

'A' is the activating event: Activating events are the experiences we encounter. These events are described in factual, objective terms e.g. I stay late at work until 7pm on most weekdays.

'B' is the belief: This is where you access faulty thinking, images and beliefs.

'C is the consequent emotions: The resulting feelings experienced as a result of our interpretation of the event. Albert Ellis suggests that people differ with regard to their feelings associated with events, solely due to the fact that they have different interpretations. The following example shows two different interpretations of being made redundant:

Activating event	Belief	Consequent emotions
I am made redundant	I'm a loser	Depression
I am made redundant	I'll get a better job that is more satisfying.	Excited

We create a basic understanding of ourselves and the world around us based on our experience and learned responses. Some people engage with negative interpretations while others are able to assess most situations in a resilient manner.

Put learners in pairs, Partner A and Partner B. A is to introduce a current or recent activating event they have experienced and discuss it for 10 minutes while B uses listening and questioning skills to help A uncover related beliefs and emotions. Allow time for the pair to discuss the process between them before they change over. Then gather everyone back into the larger group to debrief.

Finally, give out copies of both handouts and ask the group to read them for homework.

 Discussion points: What was it like doing the activity? What did they discover about themselves? Which questions were particularly helpful?

Emotional intelligence

 1-2-1

Time: 30 minutes

Resources:

 Handout 4.6: Emotional intelligence

Instructions:

Using **Handout 4.6: Emotional intelligence**, give the learners a brief introduction to the concept of emotional intelligence. The areas of emotional intelligence which can help the individual manage strong emotions include self-awareness and self-regulation.

Next, ask the learners to form smaller groups to discuss the information before coming back together to discuss as a larger group. Use the discussion points below to aid the conversation if needed.

 Discussion points: What was it like doing the activity? What did you discover about yourself? Which questions were particularly helpful?

Managing anger

 1-2-1

Time: 30 minutes

Resources:

 Handout 4.3: Managing strong emotions

 PowerPoint Slide 11: Dynamics of anger

Instructions:

Show **PowerPoint Slide 11: Dynamics of anger** and read through the list of causes of anger before asking the group to volunteer other things that make them angry.

Ask the learners to refer back to **Handout 4.3: Managing strong emotions** and explain that you are going to be discussing anger management. Next, put learners into small groups to discuss how they relate to the anger management techniques from the handout before coming back into the larger group to have a wider discussion.

Techniques include:

▶ Observing, identifying and taking responsibility for your feelings.

▶ Deep breathing.

▶ Mindfulness.

▶ Feeling your feelings.

▶ Not blaming others.

▶ Talking out your feelings.

▶ Thought stoppage.

▶ Understanding how you cope with threat.

▶ Identifying the feelings hiding other feelings.

▶ Applying reason to emotion.

▶ Writing out your feelings.

▶ Sitting with negative feelings.

 Discussion points: What was it like doing the activity? What did you discover about yourself?

Managing anxiety

 1-2-1

Time: 30 minutes

Instructions:

For this activity, take the learner/s through the following information answering any questions that might arise or stimulating conversation where appropriate.

Anxiety is a state of heightened arousal in response to a real or perceived threat. Chronic anxiety could lead to more intense psychological distress or to physical symptoms. Typical symptoms of anxiety include:

Physiological:	pounding or racing heart, breathing difficulties, tremor and shaking, feeling weak, dizzy and faint, feelings of nausea, body tension and aching muscles, tingling and sweating.
Behavioural:	agitation, pacing up and down, scratching, yawning, crying, obsessive-compulsive behaviours, avoidance and withdrawal (includes over-eating, substance abuse, indecision and procrastination) – an anxious individual often seeks reassurance from others.

Emotional: panic, feelings of helplessness, powerlessness or being overwhelmed, fear (of fainting, loss of control, acting 'crazy', losing one's mind, being trapped, being negatively judged, being humiliated, being hurt, becoming sick or dying prematurely).

Cognitive: poor concentration, poor short-term recall, erratic attention, easily distracted by irrelevant stimuli, difficulty in focusing, pre-occupied with perceived 'danger', over-vigilant for danger-related signals of stimuli.

Introduce these physiological, behavioural, emotional and cognitive headings with an example or two before putting the learners into four groups, each with a heading to tease out further symptoms through further discussion.

Cognitive features also include:

▶ Distorted thinking, wrong assumptions and erroneous conclusions based on inferences and negative evaluations, faulty logic and analyses. This includes over-estimating the likelihood of negative outcomes and under-estimating personal ability to cope.

▶ Catastrophising – applying erroneous negative evaluations and falsely predicting 'disastrous' results.

▶ Selective abstraction – focusing exclusively on the negative aspects of a situation, while ignoring anything positive.

▶ Dichotomous thinking – interpreting neutral or ambiguous elements as either negative or threatening.

Below are some examples of natural anxiety management tools.

▶ **Exercise:** Your anxiety will often become much worse when you don't exercise because your muscles turn that pent up energy into physical stress, which in turn becomes mental stress. On the flipside, when you exercise, you not only reduce that extra energy but you also improve hormone balance, release neurotransmitters that improve mood and improve breathing.

▶ **Lifestyle:** Living a healthy lifestyle is important. From sleep to nutrition to hydration, the healthier your body is the better it works, and the better it works the less you'll experience anxiety.

▶ **Yoga:** Yoga is a type of exercise that has additional benefits to reducing anxiety. First, it's slower without being any less challenging, and those with anxiety need an opportunity to slow their lives down so that it feels more manageable. Yoga also teaches breathing techniques that can be very valuable for fighting anxiety.

▶ **Relaxation strategies:** Many relaxation strategies exist that can help you cope with anxiety. Visualisation is a great one. It involves imagining yourself and your five senses in a more relaxed place. These strategies give your mind an opportunity to be calmer, so that you have a chance to re-learn how to cope with stress naturally.

▶ **Distractions:** Distractions are also an important part of anxiety management. Your thoughts tend to be your enemy when you suffer from anxiety. So distractions allow you to stop focusing on those thoughts and give yourself a break to simply calm down.

▶ **Journaling:** Writing down your thoughts in a journal is a powerful coping tool. It benefits anxiety in two ways. First, it gives you a chance to simply let out your thoughts. Second, it puts your thoughts in a permanent place, and that tells your brain that it doesn't have to focus on remembering them as much as it did previously.

Depending on the time available, you could coach the learners in a simple activity chosen from these tools for them to practise at home.

 Discussion points: What was it like doing the activity? What did they discover about themselves? Which questions were particularly helpful?

Stop, drop and process

 1-2-1

Time: 45 minutes

Resources:

 Handout 4.4: Stop, drop and process

Instructions:

The stop, drop and process technique can help us manage strong emotions and to remain in control when we experience things that might otherwise overwhelm or upset us. First, explain to the learners the principles of the technique.

STOP: Stop yourself from re-acting to a feeling by focusing on your breathing, following your breath as it moves in and out of your body. Acknowledge and identify the fact that you've been strongly affected by an intense emotion. It helps to name the emotion, 'I'm feeling angry,' or, 'I'm sad'. You don't have to analyse the feeling, just acknowledge it and focus on your breathing.

DROP: When we're experiencing strong emotions, we often lose touch with our physical body. To become grounded inside your body, bring your attention to the sensation of your feet on the ground. If you're sitting, feel the contact between your body and the cushion or floor. Once you're grounded, find your emotional centre. Touch your finger to the spot on your breastbone in the centre, where you'll feel a slight hollow there. Imagine that behind this little hollow lies your inner heart, an emotional centre. Focus your attention into this emotional centre and imagine your breath going into it for a few minutes, calming and soothing you.

PROCESS: Once you have found your centre, focus again on the feeling you are working with. Where is it in your body? How does it feel? At this point, you'll notice that certain negative thoughts may be attached to your emotion. Acknowledge these thoughts and then let them go, keeping your attention on the feeling itself rather than getting caught up in your personal story line or the specific events that caused the feeling. Now that you've identified the emotion and its cause, and crucially 'dropped' its intensity to a more manageable level, this 'processing' stage essentially involves thinking, or 'processing' the emotion. Think about the events that caused your distress, ask yourself why it upset you, are there any underlying issues that need to be addressed? Then explore what steps you can take to resolve the situation.

Having outlined the above, give each leaner a copy of **Handout 4.4: Stop, drop and process**, asking them to read through it and then hold a group discussion about how this technique can be used for managing strong emotions and diffusing situations.

Next, split the group to work in threes and ask each member to take it in turn for 10 minutes to reflect on a situation in which they could have used this technique. If preferred, the learner can choose a current situation and discuss how they might apply it. Finally, gather everyone back into the larger group to debrief. Use the points below to aid the discussion if needed.

 Discussion points: How did you experience the activity? What was particularly challenging?

Feeling in the body

 1-2-1

Time: 30 minutes

Resources:

 PowerPoint Slide 12: Feeling in the body

Instructions:

Open a discussion on how we can locate feelings in the body. Ask the learners to work in pairs, each learner sharing a recent time when they felt strong emotion (10 minutes each way). Show **PowerPoint 12: Feeling in the body** and, as they reconnect with the emotion, their partner should ask the following questions:

▶ What shape is the feeling?

▶ Where exactly is it located?

▶ What colour is it, if any?

▶ What kind of texture does it have?

▶ Does it change over time?

Gather everyone back into a larger group for a wider discussion using the points below if needed.

 Discussion points: By locating our emotions in the body in this way, we realise that the emotion is smaller than we are. We're bigger than any emotion that we experience, which means that if we stand back from it we can see that not everything we're experiencing is coloured by the emotion. In this way we create a sort of 'space' between ourselves and the emotion so that we're not so caught up in it.

Circle of support

 1-2-1

Time: 15 minutes

Instructions:

Introduce this trust activity as an example of working with strong emotion. Each learner takes a turn walking for three minutes with their eyes closed in a circle made up of the rest of the group. Each participant begins by turning around a few times with their eyes closed in the centre of the circle before walking straight ahead. The rest of the group is responsible for making sure the person walking is supported and safe. Gather everyone back into the larger group for discussion using the points below if needed.

 Discussion points: What was it like walking with your eyes closed? How did you feel about trusting the group? What was it like being part of the team responsible for keeping someone safe?

Eye to eye

 1-2-1

Time: 20 minutes

Instructions:

Ask the learners to walk about the room without making eye contact with anyone else for two minutes. Give them sticky-notes to write down any feelings they may experience during this activity, which they can post on a specified place on the wall.

The group is then instructed to walk about the space in the same way for two minutes, only this time they are to seek out eye contact with others but immediately look away when eye contact is made. Feelings are again recorded on sticky-notes and placed in another spot.

The group is then instructed to walk about the space and seek out eye contact, pairing up with the first person to reciprocate. They should then walk side by side with that person for two minutes, both partners making no eye contact with anyone else. They should again be recorded on sticky-notes and placed in a third spot.

Gather the group back into a large circle with eyes cast down. On the count of three everyone looks up and seeks eye contact with someone.

Finally, discuss the exercise as a group, using the points below as needed and the sticky notes on the wall.

 Discussion points: What feelings are evoked by each stage of the exercise? What feels good, what feels bad or in between and why? In what ways does this apply to life in the real world, for example what is your emotional reaction to people who look away rather than make eye contact? What might it mean for learner/student contact to make solid eye contact? How does eye contact influence interaction?

Approach and withdraw

 1-2-1

Time: 20 minutes

Instructions:

Divide the learners into two groups facing face each other a few feet apart and set up a conflict between them, for example, going out for pizza or staying in for dinner. Each learner in turn then makes positive statements about their team's position in an effort to persuade members of both teams. When a learner finds an argument persuasive, they move closer to the person who made the statement, and when they find something discouraging about one side or the other the learner steps back from the person who made the statement.

Once this is complete, gather everyone back into a larger group to discuss the exercise using the points below if needed.

 Discussion points: What was like when members of your team moved closer to the other team but you were not persuaded? What arguments pulled you toward the other team and why?

Journal reflections and post-session practice

The learners should complete **Handout 4.2: Identifying your emotional signals** and give another copy to a work colleague, partner or friend to complete. They should record their thoughts in their journal.

If the learners did this during the session, they should read **Handouts 4.5** and **4.7** and make notes for the next session.

Unit 5: Effective questioning

Introduction

Good communication involves questioning to elicit facts and listening to identify the nub of the issue.

There are basically two types of questions: open and closed. Open questions widen out the dialogue because the other person has to give a considered answer. Closed questions, on the other hand, can be answered with a simple one word answer, often 'yes' or 'no', thus closing down the possibility of further conversation. For example, asking, 'How did you feel when you met him again after so long?' will evoke a more detailed response than, 'Did you feel happy or angry when you met him again?', a question that could be answered with a simple 'happy' or 'angry'. Again, asking someone, 'Do you think he was happy to see you?' is closed while, 'How do you think he felt seeing you after so long?' is open, and widens the range and detail of possible responses.

Without effective questioning, we may not have the clarity we need to move the communication forward in a positive way. When we do have this skill, we increase our resilience and our problem-solving skills.

Depending on group size, this unit should take about 1 hour to complete.

Aims

This unit aims to teach learners about effective questioning and how to use the skill. By the end of the session, they should:

▶ have gained an insight into how asking questions helps us to understand others

▶ know the difference between open and closed questions.

Activities

Draw what you hear

 1-2-1

Time: 20 minutes

Ask learners to get into pairs and sit back to back. One person in each pair should have a piece of paper and a pen or pencil. Give the other person in the pair an abstract drawing, for example different shapes joined up, which they have to describe to their partner. For example:

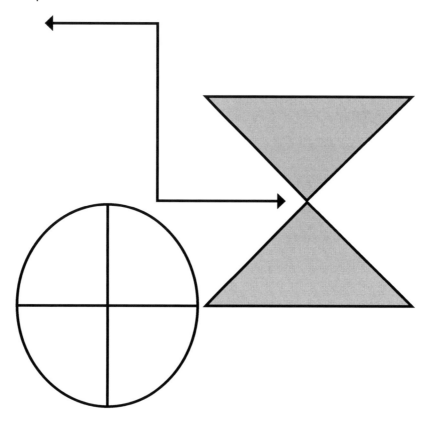

Round one: The communicator will describe a picture of assorted geometrical shapes. The listener/drawer can't ask any questions, they must just listen and draw based on what they hear.

Round two: A different picture of geometric shapes is described and the listener/drawer can only asked closed questions.

Round three: A different picture of geometric shapes is given and the listener/drawer can use open questions.

Gather everyone back into a larger group to discuss the exercise using the points below, if needed.

 Discussion points: When the time is up, ask the learners to compare the drawing to the original. Discuss why there were differences. Was it in the way an image was described or was it the listening? Was it because you couldn't ask questions to clarify what was being described? What about not being able to see the person to get the visual clues such as nodding or frowning. What about the noise in the room – is it a distraction when you want to listen to someone properly? What should you do to create a good environment for listening? How should you behave to show you are listening?

Types of questions

 1-2-1

Time: 30 minutes

Resources:

 Handout 5.1: Types of questions

 PowerPoint Slide 13: Types of questions

Instructions:

Show **PowerPoint Slide 13: Types of questions**, give out copies of **Handout 5.1** and explain that there are a range of different types of questions.

Next, ask the learners to get into pairs. One partner then chooses a subject to discuss for 10 minutes while the other asks questions using maybe five different types of question from the handout. After 10 minutes, allow time for discussion in pairs as to how they experienced the activity. Then they change roles. After 10 minutes, allow further discussion before coming back into the large group for feedback using the discussion points below as needed.

 Discussion points: Which questions opened you up most? What type of question tended to close you up?

Paper cut

 1-2-1

Time: 10 minutes

Instructions:

In order to do this exercise you will need one sheet of A4 paper for each learner; scissors are optional.

This activity explores the importance of perception and asking questions in the communication process. It aims to illustrate the importance of giving meaningful instructions to others and how clarifying can aid the correct execution of those instructions.

Explain to the learners that you are about to give them a set of instructions that they must follow. They must follow them quietly and they are not allowed to ask any questions. They should not get help from others around them or even look at other people's work. If anyone asks questions, simply tell them to follow the instructions as they see fit.

These are the instructions:

▶ Hold up the paper.

▶ Fold the paper in half.

▶ Cut (or neatly tear) off the top right corner of the folded paper.

▶ Fold it in half again.

▶ Cut off the top left corner of the paper.

▶ Fold it in half again.

▶ Cut off the bottom right corner of the paper.

▶ Fold it in half.

▶ Cut off the bottom left corner of the paper.

▶ Unfold the paper.

Ask learner's to show their unfolded papers to each other and examine similarities and differences. Use the points below to generate discussion if needed.

 Discussion points: Did you end up with similar patterns or was everyone's pattern different? Why is that? Were the instructions clear enough? What was missing? Why is feedback so critical in communication? What happens if feedback is missing? What lessons do we take from this?

Journal reflections and post-session practice

Learners could:

▶ Observe their questioning skills for one week and comment in their journals.

▶ Observe the questioning skills of others for one week and comment in their journals.

Unit 6: Active listening

Introduction

Poor listening can often lead to misunderstandings and time-wasting errors between you and others. Effective listening is therefore a key skill for the resilient communicator.

We can all hear unless we have an impairment of some sort, but listening is more sophisticated. For example, someone might say, 'I'm happy with this piece of work I've done', but if you listened to their tone of voice, how they said the words and their body language, you might pick up that they are confused and aren't feeling too confident about their work.

Active listening means you have to attend to all the signals given off by the other person, not only the sounds but also the non-verbal signals. The purpose of this active listening is to pay attention and try to understand a person's thoughts, feelings and behaviours.

Depending on group size, this unit will take approximately 2hrs 45 minutes to complete.

Aims

This unit aims to teach learners about active listening and how to use the skill. By the end of the session, they should be able to:

▶ identify what interferes with their listening skills

▶ understand how emotions can contribute to selective listening

▶ paraphrase what they have heard

▶ listen actively

▶ understand the value of silence as part of listening.

Activities

 1-2-1

Sources of interference

Time: 15 minutes

Resources:

 Handout 6.1: Sources of interference

Introduction:

Give each learner a copy of **Handout 6.1: Sources of interference** and introduce the subject of things that can interfere with listening from both the speaker and listener's perspective. Ask the learners to work in pairs to discuss the interferences listed on the handout before coming back into the larger group to discuss using the points below as needed.

 Discussion points: How do we learn our listening skills? How can you improve your listening skills? What's interfering with your listening skills right now?

Telephone

Time: 15 minutes

Instructions:

To start this exercise game, ask the learners stand to in a circle. Whisper a sentence you have prepared before the session to the first person. They continue by whispering the sentence to next person and so on. After each person hears the message, they write down what they heard. The last person to hear the message then reads the message aloud. The first person will read the sentence they were given, and learners can note how much the two have changed as it progressed around the circle. It's likely, especially in large groups, that the message has been altered. Discuss the experience as a group, and use the points below as needed.

 Discussion points: You can post the note cards up on the wall. Then the team can study how subtle changes in word use, slight additions or eliminations, can significantly alter the meaning of the message.

Selective listening

 1-2-1

Time: 15 minutes

Instructions:

Explain to the learners that selective listening is the act of hearing and interpreting only parts of a message that seem relevant, while ignoring or devaluing the rest. Often, selective listeners will form arguments before they've heard the full story, making them not only poor listeners, but poor speakers too.

List 20 related words on a particular topic, for example, sleep, and pick one word to be intermingled in the list three times, such as, the 3rd, 7th, and 12th word will be 'sleep'. Leave out one obvious word from the list such as 'bed'. Next, ask the learners to listen as you read the list to them. Once you have finished, give them one minute to write down as many of the words as they can remember.

 Discussion points: Most people will remember the word that was repeated the most, and a notable amount will most likely write down words that were obvious, but not actually stated in the list. Usually 60% will remember the first word, 75% will get the last word on your list, 80% will remember the word that was repeated three times and 20% will write down the obvious word you never said. Debrief why all this happened and what we can learn from it.

Listen and paraphrase

 1-2-1

Time: 15 minutes

Instructions:

Read a short article from a magazine or newspaper and ask the learners to paraphrase it on a piece of paper. This activity is designed to show that learners choose to interpret and prioritise certain pieces of information over others.

 Discussion points: What can influence our interpretation of what we hear? Why might we prioritise certain information?

Journey to work

 1-2-1

Time: 20 minutes

Instructions:

Ask the learners to work in pairs and write down their journey to the course in as much detail as they can, for example, 'I got into my car and turned left out of my driveway. At the end of the street, I turned right and took the second right onto the main road at the traffic lights.'

Person A should then read their journey to Person B. Person B should stop Person A when they think they have heard as much as they can accurately repeat back word for word. They should then repeat what they have heard. Person A checks whether it is accurate, and if so, they continue with the next stage of the journey. If it is not correct, they should repeat that part of the journey again until person B can recite it word perfectly. Continue until the journey is ended and the learners swap over.

Finally, gather everyone back into a larger group to discuss the exercise using the discussion points below as needed.

 Discussion points: The activity demonstrates that there are lots of distractions to effective listening, that we have a very short attention span and that we tend to put things in our own words, which can alter the meaning.

Active listening

Time: 20 minutes

Resources:

 Handout 6.2: Becoming an effective listener

 PowerPoint Slide 14: Active listening (1)

PowerPoint Slide 15: Active listening (2)

PowerPoint Slide 16: Active listening (3)

Instructions:

Give out copies of **Handout 6.2** and give the group a few minutes to read through it.

Show **PowerPoint Slide 14: Active listening (1)** and explain the following:

▶ Body language is an important component of active listening. While we may be listening to the words and tone of voice of the other person, we also need to be aware of non-verbal clues. Sometimes, what someone says and their body language are at odds. Be aware of eye contact.

▶ Observe your own blocks to listening such as mind reading, rehearsing, filtering, judging, daydreaming, advising, sparring, being right, changing the subject and placating.

▶ Be mindful that you can't listen and talk at the same time

▶ Don't give advice unless asked for it – and avoid interrupting.

▶ When engaging with active listening, ask questions to clarify what you think you heard.

▶ When we listen, we can't help but plan what we're going to say in response. Let go of your own agenda and focus all your attention on the other person speaking. Keep an open mind and don't judge. Think before you say anything in response, especially if it is an emotional reaction.

▶ Don't look for the right or wrong in what the other person is saying. Just listen.

Show **PowerPoint Slide 15: Active listening (2)** and explain the following points:

▶ Possess an attitude of respect and acceptance towards the speaker and get inside their frame of reference as much as you can by tuning into their internal viewpoint. Show your understanding of the speaker's context and difference.

▶ Send good voice messages and body messages, making sure that what is said is reflected in your body language.

▶ When speaking, use openers such as, 'How have you been getting on?' and small rewards, which are brief verbal and non-verbal expressions of interest such as, 'yes,' or, 'tell me more', as well as open-ended questions.

▶ Paraphrase occasionally e.g. summarising what the other person has said.

▶ Reflect the feelings shared by the other person e.g. 'I can hear the anger in your voice'.

Show **PowerPoint Slide 16: Active listening (3)** and explain that hearing is a one-dimensional activity while listening is a multi-faceted activity. Bearing in mind any physiological ear issues, we can all hear. However listening to another person speak is not just registering the sounds, but listening to the tone, words, pitch and pace of the speaker's voice. Active listening is deeper still as we listen to the spoken and unspoken words and observe the body language.

Divide the group into pairs, and name one partner A and the other partner B. Next, ask all the Bs to wait outside the room. Inform the A group that their partner will speak to them for three minutes but that they are not allowed to interact at all with them. They can, however, put up their hand for five seconds every time their partner says something that makes them want to ask a question or say something.

Next, inform the B group that they are to speak to their partner about something of interest to them. At the end of the three minutes ask the B group how they felt while talking to their partner (which are likely to include comments related to not feeling listened to, didn't understand why they were putting their hand up or that they lost their train of thought because they weren't listening).

Run the exercise again, this time allowing the A group partner to interact by asking questions and becoming involved in the conversation. Finally, gather everyone back into a larger group to discuss the exercise using the points below as needed.

 Discussion points: Compare the two versions to see which was found to be the most satisfying experience. Discuss differences between hearing and listening.

Space and silence

 1-2-1

Time: 20 minutes

Resources:

 Handout 6.3: Creating space and managing silence

Instructions:

Give each learner a copy of **Handout 6.3: Creating space and managing silence** with the blank side facing upwards. After a few moments, ask them to turn it over and give them five minutes to read it through. Next, ask everyone to get into pairs. They each take it turns to talk for five minutes, in the middle of which they are silent for 30 seconds. To add an extra dimension, the listener could ask the speaker a question and the speaker doesn't reply for 30 seconds.

Gather everyone back into larger group to discuss, using the points below as needed.

 Discussion points: How do you feel about silence when listening to some else? How to you feel when you fall silent in conversation? What might periods of silence in a conversation mean?

Listen

 1-2-1

Time: 30 minutes

Instructions:

Ask the learners to get into pairs, one of whom is selected as the listener and the other as the speaker. The speaker should talk about a subject for 10 minutes, and the listener must encourage them to keep talking, but they are only allowed to make three statements during the ten minutes. After 10 minutes, the pairs switch roles. When both partners have had a go, gather everyone into larger group to discuss using the points below if needed.

 Discussion points: How did the speaker feel when the person just listened and did not exchange information? How did non-verbal signals encouraged the speaker? How uncomfortable was the silence? How did it feel to listen without having the pressure to contribute? How did the speaker feel having the freedom to say whatever he/she felt?

What you're saying is...

 1-2-1

Time: 15 minutes

Instructions:

Ask the group to get into pairs and give them a topic they will debate – choose a topic that it is easy to have differing opinions, but nothing too controversial that might generate highly emotional responses or arguments. The focus should be on the skill of listening to other points of view. Here are some suggestions:

▶ I love shopping malls vs. shopping malls are awful

▶ Should laptops be allowed in classrooms?

▶ Does money motivate people more than any other factor in the workplace?

▶ Do school uniforms help to improve the learning environment?

▶ Which is the more complicated gender: men or women?

▶ What are the advantages of bottled water vs. regular water?

▶ What impact do social networking and social networking sites have on society?

▶ Are single sex schools more effective than co-ed schools?

▶ Is it effective to censor parts of the media?

Each member of the pair then shares their opinion one sentence at a time without directly responding to the other person's point, for example:

A. Shopping malls have everything you need in one place.

B. Shopping malls are energy drainers.

A. If I want to go to Smith's or Superdrug, it's all right there.

B. They waste space and are bad for the environment.

A. And you can go to lunch right there.

B. Shopping malls are crowded and noisy.

This continues for two minutes.

Next, each partner shares their opinion again, one sentence at a time, but this time the partner responds by paraphrasing that sentence without using any of the same words, starting with, 'So what you're saying is…':

A. Some of my best memories with my kids have taken place in shopping malls.

B. So what you're saying is that there are happy times you like to think about and that many of them occurred in places where shops are all inside one big building.

If A confirms that that's what they said then B shares a sentence and A paraphrases.

Gather everyone back into a larger group to discuss the exercise using the points below if needed.

 Discussion points: What was it like to try to listen to someone else at the same time as you were talking? Can you think of times when you try to listen to another person while your own thoughts are racing? What was it like to share without your partner responding to what you said? What was it like to paraphrase what your partner said? What gets in the way of representing what the person was saying? Were you aware of your own bias, judgements or perceptions interfering with simply re-stating their point?

Journal reflections and post-session practice

Before the next session, learners could:

▶ Observe their listening skills for one week and comment in their journals.

▶ Observe the listening skills of others for one week and comment in their journals.

Unit 7: Building perseverance

Introduction

Perseverance is that true grit quality whereby we stay on course until we reach our objective. This doesn't mean that we shouldn't adapt along the way – only that we don't give up.

Resilience is about returning to your centre (to balance, if you like) after being challenged by life. Perseverance is a steady persistence in purpose and action in spite of difficulties. Becoming resilient when under distress empowers your faith and takes your perseverance to new depths. This unit helps learners unpick what perseverance means for them.

Depending on group size this unit will take approximately 4hrs to complete.

Aims

This unit aims to teach learners about building perseverance. By the end of the session, they should be able to:

▶ understand when to persevere and when to let go

▶ identify the qualities needed for perseverance.

Activities

Grit or quit?

 1-2-1

Time: 20 minutes

Resources:

 PowerPoint Slide 17: Grit or quit

Instructions:

Explain how sometimes we can persevere through to success, while there are also times to quit because it's just not coming together, maybe due to lack of skills, knowledge or support.

Ask the learners to form a circle and to share an experience of perseverance or when they decided to let go. You could ask:

▶ What made you persevere? What qualities did you use to help you persevere?

▶ What made you quit? How does quitting make you feel?

You might open a discussion on:

▶ the personal qualities and skills necessary to persevere such as determination or a support network

▶ how important is motivation?

▶ the difference between stubbornness and perseverance.

Show **PowerPoint 17: Grit or quit** and open a discussion on how we might recognise when we should hang on in there and when should we let go, asking the learners to share personal examples.

 Discussion points: Share a time in your life where you had to choose if you were going to persevere or quit? What did you choose?

At the end of your life, do you want to be able to say you 'fought the good fight and finished your race'? If so, do you think you'll need perseverance to be able to do that?

Share an experience where you feel like the fact that you persevered through a situation has built your character.

Opposite hand

 1-2-1

Time: 15 minutes

Instructions:

As an example of perseverance, explain how your brain is wired to use your dominant hand, so it takes willpower to use the opposite. Ask the learners to write a short note (no more than an A4 side) to someone they know with their non-dominant hand.

 Discussion points: How did you experience the activity? What was particularly challenging?

Perseverance

 1-2-1

Time: 15 minutes

Resources:

 PowerPoint Slides 18: Perseverance (1)

PowerPoint Slide 19: Perseverance (2)

Show **PowerPoint slide 18** and ask the learners to consider something in their life (past or present) that they held steadfast to or are holding steadfast to.

Use **PowerPoint slide 19** and the discussion points below, if needed, to encourage a general discussion around the idea of perseverance.

 Discussion points: When you're going through a difficult time, what do you hold on to?

Small ball

 1-2-1

Time: 20 minutes

Instructions:

Have one small ball for each learner. Ask them to:

▶ take the ball in one hand and pass it around their waist, changing hand as appropriate to make a complete circle around their body.

▶ using both hands, take the ball and circle around each leg from top to bottom

▶ do a figure eight with the ball – around one leg, between the legs, then around the other leg

▶ drop the ball behind their back and catch it with the opposite hand.

 Discussion points: How did you experience the activity? What was particularly challenging?

Roles models

 1-2-1

Time: 15 minutes

Resources:

 PowerPoint Slide 20: Role models

Instructions:

Open a discussion on famous people who have demonstrated perseverance. Some of the ideas on **PowerPoint slide 20: Role models** may help to get things moving. You may want to prepare some information for this exercise in advance.

 Discussion points: How did you experience the activity? What was particularly challenging?

Icy perseverance

 1-2-1

Time: 15 minutes

Instructions:

Have an ice cube for each learner with a penny frozen inside. Explain that the first person to get the penny out of their ice without putting it in their mouth or hitting it with another object is the winner.

 Discussion points:

▶ How does melting the ice cube compare to reaching your goals?

▶ Did you ever feel like quitting? Why do some people quit before reaching their goals?

▶ Could you have got the penny quicker had you broken the rules?

▶ Would you feel as good about winning if you didn't follow the rules?

▶ How do hard work and perseverance help you achieve your goals?

Sink or swim?

 1-2-1

Time: 10 minutes

Instructions:

Have a clear glass bowl with water and modelling clay (not Play-Doh).

Roll the clay into four balls, three of them small and one a little larger (like small and big marbles).

Drop each small ball into the water and watch them sink. Tell the learners that each ball represents a person that feels discouraged by life's difficulties. We all feel like that at times. Just like the clay balls, you may want to give up and sink into a state of despair.

Next, take the larger clay ball and start reshaping it to form the shape of a simple boat. Talk about how this person is not going to give up when faced with a problem. They are choosing to have a positive attitude and to show perseverance.

Discuss how it's possible to work through the challenges and achieve your goal by 'reshaping' your attitude. Put the boat in the water and watch it float. Now take each small ball and put them inside the boat. Ask the learners what they think can happen when a person has a positive attitude and decides to persevere: they not only achieve their goal, but are a positive role model for others.

 Discussion points: How did you experience the activity? What was particularly challenging?

Read it out!

Time: 1 hour

Instructions:

Have the learners work in small groups to write a short parable or story on the theme of perseverance that should take about five minutes to read. Some tips:

▶ The aim of the story is to present a solid point of view that is easily identified e.g. demonstrating perseverance.

▶ It can be humorous, inspiring, thought provoking, profound or serious.

▶ One person can read it or two.

▶ You can give each member of the group a small role to speak or act out.

▶ The story needs a beginning, middle and end.

▶ Get into the meat of the story quickly. The goal is to give your audience enough information as quickly as possible.

▶ You don't have time to waste developing elements that don't matter. Avoid discussion of things in the past/future, people who aren't present, and objects that aren't relevant to the story.

▶ The story should have a rising action before reaching the climax and ending.

Allow each group to present their story to the larger group.

When everyone has read their story, get them all back into a larger group to discuss.

 Discussion points: How did you experience the activity? What was particularly challenging?

Hands of perseverance

 1-2-1

Time: 30 mintures to 1 hour

Resources:

 Handout 7.1: Hands of perseverance

Instructions:

Have enough copies of **Handout 7.1** for each member of the group. Using the handout, teach the learners to spell out the word 'perseverance' as you discuss what it means.

Then ask the learners to spell out words that represent perseverance such as 'focused', 'determined', 'resolution', 'positive', 'endurance', 'tenacity'.

 Discussion points: How did you experience the activity? What was particularly challenging?

Journal reflections and post-session practice

Observe yourself in action and note when your perseverance is high. What are your thoughts and feelings at that time? How are you behaving?

Unit 8: Developing a non-judgemental mindset

Introduction

We are bombarded by the media with images and ideas of perfection. Consequently we begin to judge ourselves against these images and others, which in turn impacts upon our self-esteem. Most of us live with pre-conceived notions of what's right and wrong and the minute we, someone or something, doesn't fit our idea of perfection we become judgmental.

We may tend to judge others than look at our own issues. Judging others tends to make us feel superior, as if we were better than them and that temporarily makes us feel good.

A non-judgemental person shows resilience through the acceptance of diversity.

This is a short unit, and it should take you about 50 minutes to complete depending on the size of the group.

Aims

This unit aims to teach learners about developing a non-judgemental mindset. By the end of the session, they should be able to clarify and challenge the emotions connected with being judgmental.

Activities

Emotional charge

 1-2-1

Time: 30 minutes

Resources:

 Handout 8.1: Remaining non-judgemental

 PowerPoint slide 21: Developing a non-judgemental mindset

Instructions:

Set the scene for how high emotions and a judgmental mindset go together before introducing the handouts and PowerPoint slide for discussion.

 Discussion points: How did you experience the activity? What was particularly challenging?

Language

 1-2-1

Time: 20 minutes

Instructions:

First, explain to the learner/s that identifying your judgmental phrases will help you become more non-judgemental during times of stress. Frequently used judgmental words we might use include: right, wrong, unfair, should, shouldn't, stupid. Ask the learners to write down typical words they use in judgement of themselves and in judgement of others.

Next, go on to explain that we can often use negative self-talk in judgement of ourselves. Phrases like: I'm bad, stupid, lazy, weak, not worth it etc. Ask the learners to:

▶ First write down typical phrases they use in judgement of themselves e.g. 'When I make a mistake, I feel ineffective.'

▶ Rewrite the phrase into a non-judgemental statement e.g. 'When I make a mistake, I look for the lesson in it.'

 Discussion points: How did you experience the activity? What was particularly challenging?

Journal reflections and post-session practice

Bring your attention to your thoughts and judgments when you are doing simple activities, like eating. Notice the thoughts you have about the food as you eat it. Don't try to counter your judgments, just notice that they are there. What type of opinion thoughts do you tend to have?

Unit 9: Developing problem-solving skills

Introduction

The capacity for effective problem-solving is critical for resilience and depends on a person having access to a range of flexible strategies for addressing conflict, seeking help, and dealing with unforeseen setbacks.

Depending on the size of the group, this unit should take you about 3hrs 30mins to complete.

Aims

This unit aims to teach learners about developing problem-solving skills. By the end of the session they should be able to:

▶ use of some of the basic skills involved in problem-solving

▶ understand the role of creative and critical thinking

▶ use the 5-step process to solve problems

▶ begin to understand the solution focused approach to problem solving

▶ improve their decision-making processes

▶ experience goal setting and action planning.

Activities

Group wide web

Time: 30 minutes

Instructions:

Divide the group into two equal teams, providing each team with a ball of string. One member of each team leaves the room. The remaining team members create a web using the ball of string. The team member is brought back blindfolded. They then need to unravel the web, while their team members give them instructions on how to retrieve the line of string. Give them a time limit for solving it. The team that manages to solve their web first, wins.

Gather everyone back into a larger group to discuss the exercise using the discussion points below.

 Discussion points: What skills did this activity develop e.g. concentration, to give instructions correctly, not crumbling under pressure? What was it like being blindfolded and having to follow instructions? What was it like to give the instructions? What was it like working in a team?

Creative and critical thinking

 1-2-1

Time: 20 minutes

Instructions:

Explain to the learner/s that critical thinking and creativity are resilient approaches related to different sides of the brain:

Right brain functions	Left brain functions
Intuition	Reasoning
Imagination	Critical thinking
Creativity	Language

Critical thinking is the objective analysis and evaluation of an issue and involves active learning. Ask the learners to identify characteristics of a critical thinker before adding in the following points.

A critical thinker will:

▶ Demonstrate a willingness to examine beliefs, assumptions and opinions against facts.

▶ Build and appraise arguments.

▶ Seek to clearly define a set of criteria for analysing ideas.

▶ Analyse and solve problems systematically rather than intuitively.

▶ Understand how ideas link together.

▶ Identify errors in reasoning.

▶ Show a willingness to ask pertinent questions and assess statements and arguments.

▶ Have the ability to suspend judgment and tolerate ambiguity.

Creativity is thought to involve a number of cognitive processes, neural pathways and emotions. Ask the learners to identify characteristics of a creative person before adding in the following points.

A creative thinker will:

▶ Daydream.

▶ Observe everything.

▶ Make time for solitude.

▶ Seek out new experiences.

▶ People-watch.

▶ Take risks.

▶ View life as an opportunity for self-expression.

▶ Follow their true passions.

▶ Lose track of time.

Ask the group to get into pairs to discuss their personal preferences and skills related to creative and critical thinking. After 10 minutes, gather everyone back into a larger group to discuss the exercise using the discussion points below.

 Discussion points: What did you discover about your creative thinking? What did you discover about your critical thinking? What are the pros and cons of either one?

The Five-Step process

Time: 30 minutes

Resources:

 Handout 9.1: A five-step process

 PowerPoint slide 22: A five-step process

Instructions:

Give out copies of **Handout 9.1: A five-step process**, show **PowerPoint 22** and introduce the five-step process of problem-solving.

Ask the learners to get into pairs, A and B. A is given 10 minutes to talk about a problem while B uses listening and questioning skills (see Units 5 and 6) to help encourage A. Allow time for feedback before they change over. Gather the pairs back into a larger group to share their experiences and to discuss the exercise using the points below if needed.

 Discussion points: What was the activity like for you? What did you learn about yourself? What needs improving and how might you go about it?

Solution-focused approach

 1-2-1

Time: 30 minutes

Resources:

 Handout 9.2: Being solution focused

 PowerPoint Slide 23: Problem-solving skills (1)

PowerPoint Slide 24: Problems-solving skills (2)

Instructions:

A solution-focused approach dispenses with problem analysis and focuses instead on learning about goals, solutions and resources.

Give everyone a copy of **Handout 9.2: Being solution focused** and a few minutes to read through it. Next, ask the learners to get into pairs and each share for 10 minutes a particular problem before their partner takes them through a solution-focused approach.

Using **PowerPoint Slide 23: Problem-solving skills (1)**, discuss the five key steps of the solution-focused approach for resilience:

1. Clarifying goals.

2. Moving towards a solution (not focusing on the problem).

3. Awareness of how improvement has come about in the past.

4. Giving positive encouragement and acknowledgement for progress (however small).

5. Highlighting strengths and resources (internal and external).

Using **PowerPoint Slide 24: Problems-solving skills (2)**, ask the learner/s to identify a problem they would like to find a solution to and work through these questions:

▶ What do I want to achieve?

▶ Is the solution, or something similar, present? Ie. have you ever achieved the solution, or something close to it, in other situations?

▶ How can I transfer this solution to my current circumstances?

▶ What resources do I have to use in this solution? How can I use these resources?

▶ What strengths do I have to use in this solution? How can I use these strengths?

▶ If 0 is no achievement and 10 is complete goal achievement, where am I on the scale right now?

▶ What did I do to get to this level?

▶ How can I do more of that?

Gather everyone back into a larger group to discuss the exercise using the discussion points below.

 Discussion points: What was the activity like for you? What did you learn about yourself? What needs improving and how might you go about it?

Making decisions

 1-2-1

Time: 30 minutes

Resources:

 Handout 9.3: Decision-making styles

 PowerPoint Slide 25: Decision-making styles

Instructions:

Show **Slide 25** and introduce the concept of decision-making styles. Explain that there four main coping strategies:

▶ **Analytical coping strategy:** You see change as a challenging puzzle to be solved by taking time to gather information and draw conclusions.

▶ **Conceptual coping strategy:** You are interested in how change fits into the big picture. You want to be involved in defining what needs to change and why.

▶ **Behavioural coping strategy:** You want to know how everyone feels about the changes ahead. You work best when you know there is support for the change.

▶ **Directive coping strategy:** You want specifics on how the change will affect you and what your own role will be during the process. If you know the rules of the change process and the desired outcome, it will be easier to achieve your goals.

Next, give out copies of **Handout 9.3: Decision making styles** for discussion in pairs, where the learners discuss their approach to decision-making from the four strategies.

 Discussion points: What was this activity like? What did you learn about yourself? What needs improving and how might you go about it?

SCAMS

 1-2-1

Time: 15 minutes

Instructions:

Creative thought can help the problem-solving cognitive process. Explain to the learners that they are going to write a series of five-word sentences using these five initial letters – SCAMS – one letter for each word. Here are a couple of examples:

▶ Senior Citizens Arrange Maximum Security.

▶ Smooching Clive Activates Mad Sarah.

▶ Sarcastic Comments Are Meant Seriously.

▶ Sleepy Cats Always Move Slowly.

▶ Special Crocuses Aid My Sleep.

▶ Spoiled Children Angered Mother Steadily.

Ask the learners to write as many sentences as possible in five minutes.

For a variation on this theme, you could ask the learners to think of another word (no longer than six letters) and use the initial letters to write a sentence.

 Discussion points: How did you experience this activity?

Key problem-solving skills

 1-2-1

Time: 30 minutes

Resources:

   Handout 9.4: Problem-solving skills

Handout 9.5: Steps to solving a problem

Introduction:

Give each learner a copy of **Handout 9.4: Problem-solving skills** and ask them to go through the list rating themselves on a scale of 1 to 10 for each strategy (1 being not so good while 10 is great). Each learner then identifies their top problem-solving skill and shares their tips with the larger group.

Next, give out copies of **Handout 9.5: Steps to solving a problem** and read through it with the group, discussing each of the steps and answering any questions. You might suggest that, as post-session practise, the learners take a problem they are currently experiencing and go through each of these steps writing down their approach/ response to each. This does not need to be a serious problem, but is an exercise simply to get them using the steps.

 Discussion points: What was this activity like? What did you learn about yourself? What needs improving and how might you go about it?

Setting goals and action planning

 1-2-1

Time: 30 minutes

Resources:

Handout 9.6: Setting goals

Handout 9.7: Action planning

Instructions:

Give a copy of **Handout 9.6: Setting goals** to each of the learners and take them through the principles of goal setting. Highlight that goals need to be based on personal performance improvement, for example losing half a stone in six weeks or learning the basics of woodworking within three months.

Next, give out copies of **Handout 9.7: Action planning** and take the learners through it, explaining the benefits and the process of action planning. Be prepared to answer any questions the group might have, and once you have been through both handouts, encourage a general discussion on the subject using the discussion points below, if needed.

 Discussion points: What did you learn about yourself? What needs improving and how might you go about it?

Journal reflections and post-session practise

For their journal reflections and post-session practise, learners could:

▶ Observe their problem-solving skills for one week and comment.

▶ Observe the problem-solving skills of others for one week and comment.

▶ Take one problem they encounter and write a log of how they overcame it using the skills they have learnt, including setting goals and action planning.

Unit 10: Improving confidence and self-esteem

Introduction

The word 'confidence' comes from the Latin *fidere*, 'to trust'. To be self-confident is to trust in oneself, and in one's ability to engage adequately with the world. A self-confident person is ready to rise to new challenges, seize opportunities, deal with difficult situations and take on responsibility.

The word esteem is derived from the Latin *aestimare* meaning 'to appraise, value, rate, weigh, estimate', and self-esteem is our cognitive and emotional appraisal of our own worth. It is the blueprint through which we think, feel and act, and reflects and determines our relation to ourselves, to others and to the world. People with a healthy self-esteem treat themselves with respect and take care of their health, community and environment. They are able to invest themselves in projects and relationships because they do not fear failure or rejection. While they may suffer hurt and disappointment, their setbacks neither damage nor diminish them. Owing to their resilience, they are open to growth experiences and meaningful relationships, are tolerant of risk, quick to delight, and are accepting and forgiving of themselves and others.

Depending on the size of your group, this unit should take about 4hrs 25 minutes to complete.

Aims

This unit aims to teach learners about improving confidence and self-esteem. By the end of the session, they should be able to:

▶ have a basic understanding of the link between thoughts, feelings and behaviours

▶ demonstrate confident body language

▶ use positive language to describe themselves

▶ create a collage of self-esteem images and words

▶ engage in positive feedback with others.

Activities

ABC

 1-2-1

Time: 30 minutes

Resources:

 Handout 10.1: Replacing negative thoughts

Handout 10.2: The ABC model

 PowerPoint Slide 26: The ABC model (1)

PowerPoint Slide 27: The ABC model (2)

PowerPoint Slide 28: Faulty thinking errors

Instructions:

Using **PowerPoint Slide 26: The ABC model (1)**, explain the idea of how our thoughts, feelings and behaviours are linked together.

Then show **PowerPoint Slide 27: The ABC model (2)** and explain the Adversities, Beliefs and Consequences sequence. You can expand on the ABC model using **Handout 10.2: The ABC model**.

Next, ask learners to identify a recent event that caused them mild distress. Using the headings EVENT, THOUGHTS, EMOTION, BEHAVIOUR, ask them to:

▶ detail the event in one sentence e.g. taking faulty goods back to the shop

▶ identify their thoughts associated with it e.g. they'll never give me a refund

▶ identify their emotions associated with it e.g. anxiety

▶ identify their behaviour e.g. passive body language

Using **PowerPoint Slide 28: Faulty thinking errors**, explain how we can engage with distorted ways of thinking that can influence how we feel and behave. Ask the learners to identify their faulty thinking styles.

Introduce the idea of negative self-talk and how this can influence our emotions and behaviours. Then, using **Handout 10.1: Replacing negative thoughts**, ask the learners to identify a current situation that is causing some distress. Ask them to identify a couple of negative thoughts in relation to the situation. Then ask them to reframe those thoughts in a more positive statement.

Discussion points: The important point is to challenge the faulty thinking e.g. the shop has a clear policy of taking back faulty goods with a receipt. You could ask learners to move into pairs to discuss their faulty thinking and how they might reframe the thoughts.

Body language

 1-2-1

Time: 30 minutes

Instructions:

Explain to the learner/s that the body language a person uses can convey a great deal about their level of confidence. For example, evasive eye contact and slumped body posture could indicate low self-esteem while positive eye contact and an upright posture can show confidence. Not only does open and assured body language improve our body language, but it also conveys an upbeat message to others.

Go through the following simple but useful techniques for improving body language:

Confidence posing: This is the use of classic confident body language, including: head up, direct eye contact, shoulders down and back. By holding an open, expansive 'confident pose' for as little as two minutes, you can actually change your body chemistry and become more confident.

Eye contact: Using a mirror, practise making eye contact with yourself, and remember to make warm and friendly eye contact with every person you to talk to today.

Smiling: Warm up your smiling muscles by doing it consciously. Remember, that keeping a smile on your face will exude positivity while also sending a signal that you are approachable.

After introducing the subject of body language, ask learners to get into pairs, A and B. Partner A talks for five minutes while using negative body language e.g. hunched shoulders, avoiding eye contact and not smiling. They then talk for a further five minutes while A uses 'power posing' – lots of eye contact, smiling, chest out and head held high. Partner B then provides feedback before they swap roles.

When both partners have had a go, gather everyone back into a larger group to discuss the exercise. Use the discussion points below if needed.

 Discussion points: What was it like to do the activity? How did they feel when they were in the different states?

I am

 1-2-1

Time: 15 minutes

Resources:

 PowerPoint slide 29: Self-esteem is…

Instructions:

Using **PowerPoint Slide 29: Self-esteem is…** introduce the learners to the definition of self-esteem:

▶ Understanding yourself/believing in yourself: we can't change what we don't know and in order to develop, we need self-awareness. As we increase in our understanding of ourselves, we can move into positive change and self-belief.

▶ Becoming your own power source: the point of power is now, not in the past or the future, but in this moment. Not wanting to sound clichéd, but you can only give away your power, no one can take it from you. Your personal power is your source of illumination in your life.

▶ Taking responsibility/making your own choices: here we have ownership. Our life, choices, decisions and actions are down to us. No one can make us do, think, feel or behave in any way other than how we choose.

Give out pens and paper and ask the learners to write a list of ten positive words about themselves, and then change them into a positive sentence starting with the word 'I'. For example, they may be a good cook, but instead of writing 'good cook' they might write 'I am a good cook'.

 Discussion points: What was it like to complete the activity? Which sentence has the most meaning for them?

Self-esteem collage

 1-2-1

Time: 30 minutes

Instructions:

Provide a large a stack of magazines and pairs of scissors. Let the learners browse their pages to find pictures that represent themselves, their talents, abilities and aspirations, and ask them to cut them out.

Next, ask each learner to share the images they chose and talk for a short while about why they chose them.

 Discussion points: What was it like to complete? What came out of it for the learner?

Self-esteem bucket

 1-2-1

Time: 15 minutes

Instructions:

Ask the learners to mentally take a plastic bucket and pretend to hammer several nails into its bottom. Next ask them to fill the bucket with water – that will be their self-esteem. Now ask them to start removing the nails which represent the hurtful comments or life experiences that have contributed to their self-esteem diminishing.

Once the bucket is completely empty, ask the learners to identify positive way ways to plug the holes – and hence improve their self-esteem. For example, exercise, a strong family, earning more money by getting a new job, starting a new business or working from home, working on their love life, and other activities they find pleasure in.

 Discussion points: The goal of this exercise is to show the learners what hurtful life experiences and the negative things others say can do to their self-esteem. Furthermore, it will show them that the only reason why people question their worth as a person is because of these experiences and negative comments, which should in turn make them feel better about themselves.

Positive self-talk

 1-2-1

Time: 15 minutes

Resources:

 Handout 10.1: Replacing negative thoughts

Handout 10.2: The ABC model

PowerPoint Slide 30: Confidence and self-esteem (1)

PowerPoint Slide 31: Confidence and self-esteem (2)

Instructions:

You now have a choice of activity, or if you have enough time you might choose to do two.

1. Discuss again the link between thoughts, emotions and behaviours, and explain the importance of identifying, challenging and reframing negative self-talk. Ask the learners to identify two negative self-talk statements in themselves and to reframe the statements with positive self-talk. Use **Handout 10.1: Replacing negative thoughts** and **Handout 10.2: The ABC model**.

2. Using **PowerPoint Slide 30: Confidence and self-esteem (1)** discuss the cycle from beliefs through to life experiences.

3. Using **PowerPoint Slide 31: Confidence and self-esteem (2)** ask the learners to discuss which of these ways of improving self-esteem they could use more wisely.

Gather everyone back into a larger group to discuss.

Positive focus group

Time: 30 minutes

Instructions:

A positive focus group is an activity that can help improve learners' self-esteem. Focusing on one person at a time, the rest of the group talks about all of the things they like about him or her. When the time is up, another person becomes the subject of the conversation. This goes on until every person in the group has been the positive focus. Next, gather everyone back into a larger group to discuss, using the points below if needed.

 Discussion points: What was it like to experience being the positive focus person? What was it like talking about another person in this way?

Same letter, different name

Time: 20 minutes

Instructions:

Have an envelope filled with the letters of the alphabet written on small slips of paper.

Divide the group into two teams and ask each team to write down all the names of the people on the other team. Once all the names are written down, select a letter of the alphabet from the envelope. Inform the teams what letter was chosen and give them two minutes to work as a team to think of a positive word or words beginning with the chosen letter that describes each person on the other team.

Once the time limit is up, bring the two teams together and ask them to each read their list to the group. For added fun and competition, you might give each team a point for every word on their list that isn't on the other team's list.

Play as many rounds of this game as you have time for. You may want to vary the rules for the activity, for example they must think of at least two words for each person on the list.

You can hold a general discussion at the end of the game or hold a short discussion after each round.

 Discussion points: How do you feel about the words that were chosen to describe you? Were you surprised by any of the words used to describe you? If so, why? How easy or hard was it to think of positive words to describe others?

Paper gift

Time: 15 minutes

Instructions:

Giving and receiving gifts is a special event – the giver expresses their care for the receiver by selecting something he or she feels will be appreciated. This activity is about giving your understanding of others to them and learning how others see you through the exchange of thoughtful gifts.

Each member of the group chooses an imaginary gift to give to each person in the group. Each gift is drawn or described on a piece of paper to be given to the recipient. The gifts should be thought out so they represent the individuals who receive the gifts. The gifts may be deep, such as courage to face life's difficulties for someone who has shared problems with the group, or they might simply be something the receiver would enjoy, such as a season gym pass.

Once everyone has completed their gifts, let one person at a time give out his/her gifts to the others. When giving the gifts, the giver should explain what the gift is and why she or he chose to give that particular gift to the individual.

When everyone has given out their gifts, discuss the activity using the points below, if needed.

 Discussion points: How did you decide what gifts to give? What did you think about the gifts you received? Do you think there was a good match between the people and the gifts they received?

What's in a name?

Time: 20 minutes

Instructions:

Distribute a piece of paper to each member of the group and ask them to write their name vertically on the paper in big letters. Next, ask them to fold their piece of paper and place it in a box. Once you have collected everyone's bits of paper, distribute them randomly back to the group, but make sure that no one gets their own sheet. After that, ask everyone to write a positive quality of the person (whose name is written on the sheet) that starts from each letter in the name. For example, for SAM, someone might could write: S - Smiling, A - Adorable, M - Modest. Once all have finished writing, ask them to read aloud their name and the words they chose.

Finally, gather everyone back into the larger group to discuss the exercise, using the points below if necessary.

 Discussion points: What was it like receiving these qualities? What was it like to give them?

Share yourself

 1-2-1

Time: 15 minutes

Instructions:

Place the learners into groups of three. Each learner has to share out loud five qualities they like about themselves and two qualities they would like to have.

When everyone has shared, get back into the larger group to discuss the exercise, using the points below if needed.

Discussion points: What was it like engaging with the activity? If there's time, you could suggest the learners discuss one of the qualities they would like to have, the perceived barriers to achieving it, and what they could do to change.

Flip-flop

 1-2-1

Time: 20 minutes

Instructions:

 Ask the group to get into pairs and give everyone a sheet of paper. Ask the learners to write 10 good things and five bad things about themselves. Once they've done this, ask everyone to exchange their sheet with their partner. Their partner then reads out the 10 good things and then offers solutions on the five bad things that have been mentioned. The other partner will do the same and convert the five bad things into good ones by giving solutions.

Gather everyone back into a larger group to discuss, using the points below if needed.

Discussion points: What was it like to have a different perspective and solution to your negative self-perception?

Journal reflections and post-session practice

▶ **The three compliments journal:** When you wake up in the morning, write down three compliments for yourself, for example: you like how your hair looks today or you're feeling particularly intelligent. Find anything that you appreciate about yourself, things that make you feel good. The goal is to focus on your positives. Write down the compliments and congratulate yourself. Then let your day go on as usual. This will allow you to encourage self-respect and have a better mental picture about your own worth.

▶ **Something nice for yourself:** A great way to improve your self-image is learning to show appreciation for yourself. Doing something nice for yourself will make you feel better about who you are, which will certainly improve your self-esteem.

Unit 11: Assertive communication

Introduction

Assertiveness is a key trait of resilience and means you:

▶ are able to stand up for your own or other people's rights in a calm and positive way

▶ are neither being aggressive nor passively accepting what is wrong

▶ express yourself effectively while also respecting the rights and beliefs of others

▶ have self-esteem and earn others' respect

▶ possess an effective and diplomatic communication style

▶ respect yourself because you're willing to stand up for your interests and express your thoughts and feelings

▶ are aware of the rights of others and are willing to work on resolving conflicts.

Depending on the size of your group, this unit will take about 5hrs 30 minutes to complete.

Aims

This unit aims to teach learners about assertive communication and how to use it. By the end of the session, they should be able to:

▶ use assertive body language

▶ say no

▶ reduce conflict

▶ gain clarity into the 'blame game'

▶ manage criticism

▶ ignore manipulation

▶ gain clarity into the 'should' statement.

Activities

Yes and no

 1-2-1

Time: 10 minutes

Instructions:

Divide the group into pairs. Each pair then sits on the floor back to back. One learner says YES and pushes while the other says NO and pushes back. This activity explores the power of the YES and NO word.

Get everyone back into a larger group to discuss, using the points below if needed.

 Discussion points: What was like to say yes? What was it like to say no? How did the pushing influence you?

Know yourself

 1-2-1

Time: 20 minutes

Resources:

 PowerPoint Slide 32: Benefits of being assertive

PowerPoint Slide 33: Myths about assertiveness

Instructions:

Being assertive is about understanding that you have value and that your opinion matters, and it's about avoiding being passive and expressing yourself forcefully but, crucially, without being aggressive. Explain that the following activity is designed to help learners understand themselves and how they deal with others better.

Ask the learners about the benefits of being assertive and back up contributions using **PowerPoint Slide 32: Benefits of being assertive**.

Ask the learners about the myths of being assertive (giving one or two examples) and back up contributions using **PowerPoint Slide 33: Myths about assertiveness**.

Give each member of the group a piece of paper and a pen and ask them to draw a self-portrait, including how they would describe themselves in just eight words. When they have finished the activity, ask them to share their ideas and drawings in small groups. After they see each other's work, ask them to share their drawings with the larger group. Have the drawings posted on a wall and ask everyone to write something positive on each picture.

Finally, gather everyone back into the larger group to discuss, using the points below if needed.

 Discussion points: To what extent did you use positive or negative words in the description? What was it like to write positives on someone else's portrait? What was it like having someone write a positive on your definition of yourself?

Verbal and non-verbal cues

 1-2-1

Time: 45 minutes

Resources:

 Handout 11.1: Assertive body language

Handout 11.2: Language of assertiveness

 PowerPoint Slide 34: The mirroring and matching technique

PowerPoint Slide 35: Eye contact

PowerPoint Slide 36: Body posture (1)

PowerPoint Slide 37: Speaking assertively

PowerPoint Slide 38: Hand gestures and facial expression

PowerPoint Slide 39: Body posture (2)

PowerPoint Slide 40: Do you have leakage?

Instructions:

Explain to the group that how we communicate with our body is often in conflict with what we express verbally. Alongside our verbal communication, we are constantly giving non-verbal signals through our gestures, facial expressions, eyes and body movements. We learn more from someone's body language than we do from what they are saying, and while our mouths may lie, our bodies cannot.

Show **PowerPoint Slide 34: The mirroring and matching technique** and explain that you can influence others to change their negative postures by matching certain aspects of their posture and body language before gradually changing your posture. They will subconsciously pick up on your positive body language and begin to mirror it without thinking.

Next, give out copies of **Handout 11.1: Assertive body language** and explain that there are a range of body language techniques that people can use to increase their assertiveness. Ask them to read this handout carefully as part of their homework. Show **PowerPoint Slide 35** and say that maintaining eye contact is a vital part of being assertive. However, point out that there is a difference between maintaining natural eye contact and staring, which could be considered aggressive.

Show **PowerPoint Slide 36** and explain that they will feel more assertive if they are standing up. Draw the learners' attention to the test in **Handout 11.1** that suggests trying making a difficult phone call while standing up and noticing what difference that makes.

Show **PowerPoint Slide 37** and explain that assertive body language should be accompanied by clear, audible and firm speech. If a person's body language is assertive this will come more naturally – it is very difficult to speak passively or timidly when maintaining an assertive posture and good eye-contact. Draw the learners' attention to the tables on the handout that list the kinds of voice tones and patterns of speech that tend to accompany different types of body language. When everyone has had a few minutes to look at these tables, give out copies of **Handout 11.2: Language of assertiveness** and suggest that they review these phrases and practise using them in their own time.

Next, show **PowerPoint Slide 38** and explain that it can be useful to use hands and facial gestures. Some people are not very 'talkative' with their hands, while others use them all the time as a continuation of their verbal conversation, helping them to express all that they want to. There is no need to go over the top and wave your hands all over the place, but they don't need to be glued to your hips either.

Show **PowerPoint Slide 39** and explain that keeping an open body posture is also vital to being assertive. Crossing your arms or legs can appear defensive or afraid.

Finally, show **PowerPoint Slide 40**. These are some examples of things that should be avoided. Take the learners through each of them before asking if anyone has any questions or, if you have time, reflecting on what has been learnt in this session, using the discussion points below if needed.

 Discussion points: How do you show assertive, aggressive or passive body language?

Assertiveness game

Time: 15 minutes

Resources:

PowerPoint Slide 41: Aggressive behaviour

PowerPoint Slide 42:Passive-aggressive behaviour

PowerPoint Slide 43: Passive behaviour

Instructions:

Show **PowerPoint Slide 41**, **42** and **43** and take the group through each one to highlight the differences between aggressive, passive-aggressive and passive behaviours.

Next, explain that you're going to be doing an activity that will help the learners explore the differences between aggressive, passive and assertive approaches. Ask for a volunteer who believes they are assertive and give them an object such as a piece of fruit, a stapler, or something else you have to hand. Next, select three other individuals from the group and take them out of the room one at a time. Tell one person to use aggression to get the fruit, another to use passive techniques to get the fruit, and then tell the third to use assertive behaviour.

Finally, have a group discussion about the activity using the points below.

Discussion points: How did it make you feel being on the end of aggressive behaviour? How did it make you feel being on the end of passive behaviour? What was it like being the aggressor? What was it like being passive?

Saying no

1-2-1

Time: 30 minutes

Resources:

Handout 11.3: How to say no

Handout 11.4: Assertive responses

PowerPoint Slide 44: Assertive techniques (1)

PowerPoint Slide 45: Assertive techniques (2)

PowerPoint Slide 46: Assertive techniques (3)

Instructions:

Introduce the saying 'no' technique using **Handout 11.3: How to say no**. Put learners in groups of three and ask them to practice one of the techniques from the sheet. A is the person practicing the technique with B. C provides constructive feedback to A. Everyone has a turn at being A. Each person has five minutes to practice.

Introduce **Handout 11.4: Assertive responses**. Working in pairs, ask each learner to practise making an assertive response using one of the scenarios in the handout.

Next, using **PowerPoint Slide 44: Assertive techniques (1)**, open a discussion on:

▶ How to describe a situation in practical terms.

▶ Using the 'I' statement.

▶ How to present changes you'd like made in a specific way.

Using **PowerPoint Slide 45: Assertive techniques (2)**, open a discussion on:

▶ What it means to empathise.

▶ What it means to validate.

▶ How to state a problem clearly without waffling.

▶ How to state what you want without sounding aggressive or apologetic.

Using **PowerPoint Slide 46: Assertive techniques (3)**, open a discussion on:

▶ How to express feelings when being assertive.

▶ Not using blame.

Learners could then do an activity in pairs where they describe a current situation, their feelings about it and what changes they would like to see happen, ensuring they use the 'I' statement.

 Discussion points: How did it feel using this technique? What could you have done differently?

Fogging

 1-2-1

Time: 30 minutes

Resources:

 Handout 11.5: Special techniques

Instructions:

Give out **Handout 11.5: Special techniques** and explain that this handout covers a range of different techniques, each of which you're going to cover over the next few activities.

Explain that fogging, the first technique on the handout, is a way to reduce conflict or deflect negative or manipulative criticism by agreeing in part with someone else, but holding back from agreeing entirely – acknowledging some of the facts another might be saying, but retaining the right to choose your behaviour. For example:

Mary: You're never home when you say you're going to be.

John: I agree I'm sometimes a bit late, but normally only by ten minutes.

Put learners in groups of three to practise the technique using one of the following scenarios:

▶ You told me you'd have that report done as quickly as possible.

▶ You're lazy!

▶ You always take ages to get ready.

▶ You'd suit the blue shirt much better.

Person A is the one practising the technique with person B. Person C provides constructive feedback to A. Everyone has a turn at being A. Give each person five minutes to practise the technique before getting everyone back into larger group to discuss, using the points below if needed.

 Discussion points: How did it feel using this technique? What could you have done differently?

Broken record

 1-2-1

Time: 20 minutes

Resources:

 Handout 11.5: Special techniques

Instructions:

Explain that the next technique from **Handout 11.5: Special techniques** that you'll be looking at is the broken record.

Explain that this essentially involves repeating your point over and over using a low level, pleasant voice without getting pulled into arguing or trying to explain yourself. This lets you ignore manipulation, baiting and irrelevant logic. For example, imagine you're taking something back to a shop but the sales assistant first questions your decision, implying that there's something wrong with you for changing your mind and tells you that she can only give a credit note, etc. Using the broken record technique, you simply say, 'I have decided I don't need this and I'd like my money back'. Then, no matter what the sales assistant says, you keep repeating, 'I have decided I don't need this and I'd like my money back'. If she doesn't get it, ask to speak to a manager and say the same thing.

Put learners into groups of three to practise the technique using one of the following scenarios:

▶ Taking a book back to the shop and wanting a refund.

▶ Saying no to a neighbour who wants you to house sit her dog.

▶ Saying no to your sister coming to stay.

▶ Taking on yet more work from your boss.

Person A is practising the technique with person B. Person C provides constructive feedback to A. Everyone has a turn at being A. Each person has five minutes to practice. Back into larger group to debrief.

 Discussion points: How did it feel using this technique? What could you have done differently?

Positive reinforcement

 1-2-1

Time: 20 minutes

Resources:

 Handout 11.5: Special techniques

Instructions:

An excellent way of dealing with difficult situations is using positive reinforcement. This might be praise, a thank you or an action such as a hug.

Sometimes positive reinforcement may not work, and you'll need to use negative reinforcement which happens when a stimulus is removed after a behaviour is exhibited. The likelihood of the behaviour occurring again in the future is increased because of removing/avoiding the negative consequence. For example, a child can leave the table when they have eaten three mouthfuls of carrots, or your partner does the washing up in order to stop you telling him how often he doesn't do the dishes.

Ask the learners to identify a change they would like someone to make e.g. taking the rubbish out more often, tidying their room. Then ask them to write three statements or actions that could be used as positive reinforcement when that desired change of behaviour occurs.

 Discussion points: What do you think about using negative and positive reinforcement (with adults, with children)?

Defusing

 1-2-1

Time: 20 minutes

Resources:

 Handout 11.5: Special techniques

Instructions:

The next technique we're going to look at is the defusing technique. This simply involves acknowledging someone's side of an argument and letting them cool down before discussing the issue. For example, you might say, 'I can see that you're upset and I can understand part of your reaction. Let's talk about this later.' If they try to stay with it, you always have the right to walk away.

Put learners into groups of three to practice the technique using one of the following scenarios:

▶ You're upset your partner is going to the pub with their mates for the third time this week.

▶ Your friend fails to pay you back £50 they owe you for the third time.

Person A is the person practising the technique with person B while person C provides constructive feedback to A. Everyone has a turn at being person A. Each person has five minutes to practice.

When everyone's had a go, get them all back into larger group to discuss, using the discussion points below if needed.

Discussion points: How did it feel using this technique? What could you have done differently?

Content to process

 1-2-1

Time: 30 minutes

Resources:

 Handout 11.5: Special techniques

Instructions:

Ask the learners to look at the next item on **Handout 11.5: Special techniques**. This is the technique called 'content to process'. This technique should be used if the person you're talking to isn't listening, for example, or is deflecting the conversation onto other matters or using humour inappropriately. It essentially involves breaking away from the conversation and drawing attention to the way they're behaving. You might, for example, say, 'You're getting off the point and I'm starting to feel a bit frustrated', or, 'You don't seem to be listening, can you pay attention to what I'm saying please?' or, 'You're not taking this seriously – is this a bad time to talk?'

Ask the learners to get back into groups of three to practice the technique using one of the following scenarios:

▶ Your partner keeps making excuses to avoid the washing up.

▶ Your friend keeps turning up on your doorstep uninvited.

Person A is the person practising the technique with person B while person C provides constructive feedback to person A. Everyone has a turn at being person A. Each person has five minutes to practice.

When everyone's had a go, get them all back into larger group to discuss, using the discussion points below if needed.

 Discussion points: How did it feel using this technique? What could you have done differently?

Assertive Inquiry

 1-2-1

Time: 15 minutes

Resources:

 Handout 11.5: Special techniques

Instruction:

The next item on **Handout 11.5** is the assertive inquiry technique. Explain that sometimes an argument will break out about one thing, when in fact the real issue lies elsewhere. Establishing precisely what the problem is can be crucial to finding a solution. This technique is similar to the content to process shift and involves stopping a conversation into order to assess the real cause of an argument. For example, you might say, 'Hold on, how did we get into this argument?'

Draw the learners' attention to the example in the handout in which someone asks a colleague for help with a task. A problem occurs when the colleague appears distracted and they begin to argue. After a while, one of them stops and asks how they got into the argument, and it transpires that timing was the issue – their colleague was distracted because his mind was on his own tasks. With this realisation, they can agree to work together at a time that suits them both.

Put learners in groups of three to practice the technique. A is the person practicing the technique with B. C provides constructive feedback to A. Everyone has a turn at being A. Each person has five minutes to practice. Back into larger group to debrief.

 Discussion points: How did it feel using this technique? What could you have done differently?

The self-defeating 'should'

 1-2-1

Time: 30 minutes

Resources:

 Handout 11.6: The self-defeating 'should'

Instructions:

Explain to the learners that we often use the word 'should' in quite a negative way, both on ourselves and each other. It can become a substitute for assertiveness by instead 'guilting' someone into doing something.

These are some of the ways we use the word should:

▶ I/you should be working or studying.

▶ I/you should have called.

▶ I/you should be making more money.

▶ I/you should love my/your husband or wife.

▶ I/you should have done it differently.

▶ I/you should be a better (more competent, etc.) person.

▶ I/you should have taken out the rubbish/done the washing up.

▶ I/you shouldn't be so negative.

Explain that we learn at a young age to use the word 'should' to make ourselves feel guilty. We say things like, 'I should be studying' when we're at the pub, for example, or 'I shouldn't be doing this…' when tucking into a slice of cake.

In the first example, by saying 'should' we achieve three things:

1. We make ourselves feel bad about not studying (a just punishment).

2. We allow ourselves justify not studying – it's OK because we have been punished for our transgression (see point 1).

3. We get to stay at the pub.

However, in this example we don't tend to enjoy the pub as thoroughly as we might if we hadn't gone through this punishment chain. Feeling bad justifies our behaviour when it doesn't seem to be goal productive.

There are a number of techniques we can use to empower ourselves:

▶ To avoid the bad feelings associated with the word 'should', substitute either 'am going to' or 'will be'. So 'I should take out the rubbish' becomes 'I will (or I am going to, etc.) take out the rubbish'.

▶ When talking with others, avoid 'should'. Explain what you want and ask directly for their co-operation. Instead of saying, 'You should take out the rubbish', try, 'The rubbish bin is full – would you mind taking it out, please?' The person may say no but will probably add the reasoning behind their decision to say no ('No! I'm in the bathroom now'). You then have a choice – take out the rubbish yourself if that is your highest priority, or wait to ask someone else to perform the task.

▶ When you're saying something should or shouldn't happen, stop yourself and ask whether you want the event to happen or not. If you are saying, 'I should have washed the car,' finish the statement with something realistic like 'and I didn't', rather than 'and I am bad for not doing what I promised'. Then ask yourself if you really want the car washed, and if so, do you really want to wash it now rather than doing some other activity. This gives you the opportunity to become clear about tasks, establish priorities and make choices about your behaviour.

▶ Beware of others who say 'should' to you. Before you respond, ask yourself if you really want to do what they are asking you to and make an active choice – don't just act out of guilt because they said 'should'.

Finally, give out copies of **Handout 11.6: The self-defeating 'should** for the learners to take away with them, and have a discussion on what they have learned.

Blame statement

 1-2-1

Time: 30 minutes

Resources:

 Handout 11.7: Blame

Instructions:

Give out copies of **Handout 11.7: Blame** and explain to the learners that we can sometimes use blame inappropriately, both with ourselves and others.

When we think of somebody as being to blame for a situation we are judging their behaviour, them as a person and possibly assigning guilt. We grow up learning this process of blame, guilt, punishment and absolution, and apply it to others and ourselves through our self-talk. For example, 'She was driving the car when it broke down. It's her fault. She drives badly. I won't let her take the car out again.' The message tends to be one that implies some unpleasant consequence following the establishment of blame. But punishment is not always an effective means of changing behaviour, feelings and thoughts.

What gets lost in the process of blaming someone is most often the fundamental reason for initiating the process at the outset – that is, a person has exhibited a behaviour that has had an effect we do not like. The objective is for that person (and we may be that person) to change his or her behaviour in such a way that the new behaviour will likely result in our experiencing a more favourable consequence.

By establishing blame we focus on establishing guilt rather than on changing behaviour. We can change our blame-establishing behaviour by seeking to replace the behaviour pattern with one that may get us closer to our objective.

Discussion points: What difference does establishing blame make? How will establishing blame change anything that is happening or has happened? How will establishing blame change the behaviour of the responsible person?

Managing criticism

 1-2-1

Time: 30 minutes

Resources:

 Handout 11.8: Giving and receiving criticism

Instructions:

When providing constructive criticism to others:

▶ keep your comments specific and provide the person with some valuable information

▶ be sure the criticised behaviour is actually something that can be changed and help the other person to understand exactly what needs to change

▶ don't shame, humiliate or blame the person

▶ speak calmly and don't let your emotions dictate the conversation

▶ inform them of any benefits that might come out of acting on your suggestions

▶ time your criticisms well.

When receiving criticism:

▶ Avoid using sarcasm and put-downs. If you have a tendency to counter attack, make sure you do not respond immediately to criticism. Let the critic know that you have heard their view and would like to consider it before responding. This will give you time to gather your thoughts and respond calmly and objectively.

▶ Ask them to discuss any problems they have with your performance or behaviour.

▶ Ask them to give you time to consider them before any discussions.

Using copies of **Handout 11.8: Giving and receiving criticism**, open a discussion around any of these points:

▶ The difference between constructive criticism and destructive criticism.

▶ How they see themselves giving criticism and how they might improve their skills.

▶ How they see themselves receiving criticism and how they might improve their skills.

Journal reflections and post-session practice

Learners could practice using some of the following techniques:

▶ Saying no.

▶ Fogging.

▶ Broken record.

▶ Positive reinforcements.

▶ Defusing.

▶ Content to process.

▶ Assertive inquiry.

Unit 12: Fostering self-care

Introduction

Self-care is provided for you, by the resilient you. It's about identifying your own needs and taking steps to meet them. It is taking the time to do some of the activities that nurture you. Basically, self-care can help you feel healthy, helps you recharge and prepares you to take on your work and responsibilities.

Self-care is not just the physical, but the psychological, emotional, social and spiritual components of your well-being. You know the signs that you need to take better care of yourself when:

▶ You feel mentally or physically exhausted, overwhelmed or stretched too thin.

▶ Friends and family tell you you're working too hard, or you have to remind yourself to take a break.

▶ You've worked a 60-hour plus week.

▶ You missed out on something important you wanted to do.

▶ You get recurring infections.

▶ You go without sleep, regular meals or exercise to get more into your day.

Depending on the size of your group, this unit should take about 1 hour.

Aims

This unit aims to teach learners about fostering self-care. By the end of the session, they should have an insight into how they might improve their physical, psychological, relationship and spiritual self-care.

Activities

 1-2-1

Self-care

Time: 1 hour

Resources:

   Handout 12.1: Fostering physical self-care

Handout 12.2: Fostering psychological self-care

Handout 12.3: Fostering relationship self-care

Handout 12.4: Fostering spiritual self-care

Handout 12.5: Self-care plan

   PowerPoint Slide 47: Fostering self-care

Show **PowerPoint Slide 47: Fostering self-care** and explain to the learners that there are a number of life areas that need nurturing and caring for in order to maintain resilience: physical, psychological, spiritual and relationships.

Give out copies of each of the handouts 12.1 to 12.4 and ask the group to go through each of them, putting a tick by any activities they do regularly and highlighting any that they feel they don't do enough of, or at all.

Next, give out copies of **Handout 12.5: Self-care plan** and ask the group to complete each area with some of the items they identified might help them.

   Discussion points: What were the key findings for the learners?

Journal reflections and post-session practice

Learners could identify and implement two new self-care activities for one week and comment.

Unit 13: Improving self-compassion

Introduction

We rarely think about showing ourselves kindness. If we do, we worry that doing so is selfish or arrogant. However, self-compassion has been linked to greater well-being and resilience.

Having self-compassion means taking responsibility. Support and self-encouragement act like nurturing parents so that even when you don't do well, you're still supportive and accepting of yourself. Self-compassion focuses on changing behaviours that are making you unhappy.

This is a short unit and, depending on the size of your group it should take about 1 hour 15 minutes to complete.

Aims

This unit aims to teach learners about improving self-compassion. By the end of the session they should be able to show more kindness to themselves.

Activities

Writing yourself a letter

 1-2-1

Time: 30 minutes

Instructions:

Ask the learners to consider an issue that tends to make them feel bad about themselves, such as a mistake they've made, their appearance, any relationship issues they may be experiencing, etc.

Next ask them to imagine they have a friend who is wise, loving and compassionate, who can see all your strengths and weaknesses, including what you don't like about yourself. This friend recognises the limits of human nature, and is kind, accepting and forgiving. Write a letter to yourself from the perspective of this friend, focusing on the perceived inadequacies you tend to judge yourself for. What would this friend say to you from the perspective of unlimited compassion? And if you think this friend would suggest possible changes you could make, how might these suggestions embody feelings of care, encouragement and support?

Gather everyone into a group to discuss the exercise, using the question points below if needed.

 Discussion points: How did you experience the activity? What was particularly challenging?

Self-compassion scan

 1-2-1

Time: 15 minutes

Instructions:

Ask the learners to identify an issue in their lives that causes them emotional discomfort, such as anxiety or disappointment. Emotions are made up of physical sensations and our mind's interpretation of those sensations. These physical sensations are most often felt in our stomach, chest, throat and eyes, and can relate to different emotions. For example, a clenched stomach may be fear. A stinging sensation when we're resisting crying, can be related to any intense emotion, not just sadness, including anger or happiness. A dry mouth is associated with fear. Feeling tightness in the chest is related to sadness or grief. We often touch the area of our bodies where we are feeling intense emotions e.g. clutching our throat when we're afraid or our head when we feel like it's going to explode with frustration.

Take the participants through an exercise in which they notice where they feel the emotional discomfort physically in their bodies, and ask them to make contact with the sensations as they arise in their body. Ask them to say to themselves:

▶ I am aware of feeling hurt (this is mindfulness).

▶ I am not alone. We all struggle from time to time (this is shared experience).

▶ May I give myself the compassion I need at this time (this is self-kindness).

The learners could create their own affirmations or mantras.

Afterwards, gather everyone back together and discuss the exercise, using the points below if needed.

 Discussion points: How did you experience the activity? What was particularly challenging?

Daily self-compassion

 1-2-1

Time: 30 minutes

Resources:

 Handout 13.1: Daily self-compassion

Handout 13.2: When to use self-compassion

 PowerPoint Slide 48: Improving self-compassion

Instructions:

Show **PowerPoint Slide 48: Improving self-compassion** and explain that self-compassion consists of three components:

▶ **Mindfulness:** observing life as it is, in the moment and without judgment.

▶ **Shared experience:** when we're struggling, we tend to feel isolated and believe we're the only ones to experience loss, make mistakes, feel rejected or fail. However it's these very struggles that are part of our shared experience as humans.

▶ **Self-kindness:** being kind, gentle and understanding with yourself during times of distress.

Ask the learners to get into small groups and to identify as many ways as they can in which they could be more self-compassionate. Give out copies of **Handout 13.1: Daily self-compassion** and read through it with the group and see how many of these ideas they identified.

Next, give out copies of **Handout 13.2: When to use self-compassion** and open a discussion on self-compassion in daily life and when it could be used.

Finally, hold a discussion about the exercise, using the points below if needed.

 Discussion points: How did you experience the activity? What was particularly challenging?

Journal reflections and post-session practice

Pay close attention to your self-compassion and write in your journal each time you practise one of the techniques in **Handout 13.1: Daily self-compassion**. Ideally, they should strive to practise one technique every day.

Unit 14: Changing perspectives

Introduction

You will be familiar with the idiomatic expression about half a glass of water and how it will appear 'half full' to an optimist, while a pessimist will view that same glass as 'half empty'. Essentially, this phrase is attempting to convey that an object or a situation can appear quite different to two observers depending on their perspective. The first statement, that the glass is half full, is a positive expression, while the statement that the glass is half-empty is negative.

The reasons that make one person more or less optimistic than another are beyond the scope of this book. However, the fact is that, while people may move from one state to another depending on a wide variety of factors, unfortunately many of us take a negative perspective by default – the glass half-empty approach. Such a person will look at a situation and expect the worst, or will not take a proactive step in their life because they presume it will be unsuccessful.

Being able to change perspective is a resilient trait and helps the individual embrace not only the difficult times, but to look beyond with a positive mindset to possible solutions.

Depending on the size of the group, this unit will take about 45 minutes to complete.

Aims

This unit looks at what we can do to consciously shift our focus from the negative to the positive. It will teach a range of techniques that the learner will use to move out of a 'feeling mode' to a 'thinking mode', and how to start viewing the world around them in more optimistic terms.

Activities

 1-2-1

Move around

Time: 30 minutes

Resources:

 PowerPoint Slide 49: Changing perspective

Instructions:

Show **PowerPoint Slide 49: Changing perspective** and read through it with the group to introduce them to the unit. Highlight that we are all different and it's quite common for two or more people to look at the same thing, object or situation, and come to wildly different conclusions or to have very different perceptions of it. Point out that, if different people can hold such different points of view, it's quite possible for a person to be able to shift their own perspective and to begin to see things differently. If they have a habitually negative view point, they can train themselves to see things more positively.

Next, ask the learners to make some notes about their surroundings. When they have had five minutes or so to do this, they should all stand and move one seat to the right and sit down again. An extra empty chair needs to be placed to the right of the last person on the right before that part of the exercise begins.

When the learners sit down, they are to make notes about their surroundings as seen from their new seat, and to observe how the surroundings have been affected by this change of perspective caused by moving one seat to the right.

Hold a discussion on the exercise, using the points below if needed.

 Discussion points: How little does it takes to change one's perspective and how easy can it be to understand the perspective of others?

More than meets the eye

 1-2-1

Time: 15 minutes

Resources:

 PowerPoint Slide 49: Changing perspective

PowerPoint Slide 50: More than meets the eye

Instructions:

Show **PowerPoint Slide 50: More than meets the eye** and ask them to consider the image.

The question usually asked in connection with this design is whether they can see a vase or two human profiles. A mentally flexible person will see both. Have a show of hands to see who saw which first.

Explain that, whichever they see, or saw first, it's just a matter of perspective and that a slight mental shift completely changes the nature of the image.

Next, ask the learners to see as many additional things in the picture as they can. Ask them to look at it from as many different perspectives as they can.

 Discussion points: Additional possible answers: coffee table – candle stick – two people staring each other out in front of a blackboard – overpass pillar on a motorway – cocktail glass – piano stool – two babies laying face to face – minute-timer – chess piece – fruit holder – bird bath – sundial – chalice – keyhole – operating table.

Journal reflections and post-session practice

Practice changing perspective as much as you can during the next week using these simple activities:

▶ Listen to an argument from the other side.

▶ Lighten up.

▶ Find the positive in where you are at the moment.

▶ Ask if the issue will matter in five years' time.

▶ Say yes more often.

Unit 15: Improving adaptability

Introduction

Being adaptable means being flexible when things change. An adaptable person is one who is open to new ideas and concepts. Adopting a flexible approach to life is more likely to enable us to achieve success than maintaining a rigid outlook. Mental agility of this kind enables us to be resilient as problem solvers.

This is a single-activity unit, and depending on the size of the group it will take you about 30 minutes to complete.

Aims

This unit aims to teach learners about improving adaptability. By the end of the session, they should be able to identify ways they can adapt to changing conditions more easily.

Activities

Personal adaptability

 1-2-1

Time: 30 minutes

Resources:

 Handout 15.1: Personal adaptability

 PowerPoint Slide 51: Improving adaptability

Instructions:

It is our personal adaptability characteristics that enable us to deal with disruption. Being adaptable also offers the possibility that, not only might we survive change, but we might actually thrive during periods of turbulence. Some characteristics of adaptability include:

▶ *Talking to yourself:* When you start to think negatively, flip your mental switch to positive self-talk.

▶ *Asking questions:* Ask questions to open you up to new possibilities and create a more adaptable mindset.

▶ *Eliminating the concept of wrong beliefs from your life:* Become more aware of your judgemental thoughts regarding what is right and wrong, and become more tolerant of beliefs different to your own. Our natural habit is to align ourselves with others and work to convince (or ignore) those whose opinions differ. This means there's no way to learn from what their perspective might teach you. Hold back on forming an opinion and instead actively listen to the person. Keep asking yourself if you're wrong or whether you're missing something?

▶ *Considering the bigger picture:* Our inclination is to pull things apart and solve the little bits one at a time. However, when things are moving fast it can be more useful to look at the interactions between the minutiae for patterns. See what balance you can strike between the different parts of the problem and the larger picture of all the parts.

▶ *Resourcefulness:* You can take away a person's resources but you can't remove resourcefulness. Rather than getting stuck on one solution to solve a problem, adaptable people have a contingency plan in place for when plan A doesn't work.

▶ *Experimenting:* When it's time to act, we often nudge the process in the direction we desire. Instead of going for the tried and tested, embrace experimentation and learning.

▶ *Seeing opportunity not failure:* To adapt is to grow and change. In order to change you must let go of 'right and wrong' perceptions and adapt to new potential. Consider the habits that have defined your success in the past and question whether or not those habits will continue defining your success in the future.

Either of the following activities will help learners identify the skills they need in order to become more adaptable:

1. Putting the learners into small groups and using **Handout 15.1: Personal adaptability** as a guide, ask the learners to identify one strategy they could use to improve their adaptability:

   ▶ Trying something new – engaging with a fresh mindset or new behaviour can bring in a freshness which invigorates our creativity.

   ▶ Questioning our thoughts and behaviours – habitual responses can be limiting and it can be enlightening to question our thoughts and behaviours to ensure they are in line with what we truly feel at this moment.

   ▶ Planning to be spontaneous – security and routine are all well and good, but occasionally we need to 'break out' in an almost child-like way in order to find an even better answer.

   ▶ Deliberately trying to think in different ways – sometimes we can be fixated on a particular outcome and need to open our perspective out to a possible better outcome or solution.

Limited adaptability may cause difficulties with the following:

▶ Solving problems creatively and adapting to changing circumstances.

▶ Dealing with uncertain, unanticipated or unpredictable personal or professional situations.

▶ Learning new tasks, technologies and procedures.

▶ Interpersonal adaptability e.g. adapting interpersonal behaviour to work with others.

▶ Cultural adaptability requiring the ability to perform effectively in different environments.

▶ Demonstrating physically oriented adaptability e.g. to heat, noise.

2. Ask each learner to rate themselves (1 – needs improvement, 2 – fair and 3 – good) for the following:

Characteristic	Your rating
Optimistic? E.g. experience hope and faith	_____
Structured? E.g. able to plan	_____
Self-assured? E.g. in control of change	_____
Pro-active? E.g. takes action to make change happen	_____
Focused? E.g. able to prioritise and purse a goal	_____
Willing to seek support? E.g. values the guidance of others	_____
Open to ideas? E.g. exploratory and decisive	_____

 Discussion points: Using **PowerPoint Slide 51: Improving adaptability**, open a discussion on:

▶ **Trying something new.** Mental adaptability is aided by novelty, which contributes to brain growth and development.

▶ **Questioning your thoughts and words.** Become aware of what you're thinking and saying. Dispute those thoughts and words that don't serve you. Then substitute them with more positive concepts and words.

▶ **Increasing spontaneity.** Change your regular routine. Once in a while alter the order of your day.

▶ **Mixing up the way you think.** Creative ideas often arise after periods of focused thought and diffuse attention. So allow time to concentrate on projects or challenges both in a deliberate manner and in an unfocused way while you're doing something else.

Journal reflections and post-session practice

▶ **Try something new:** Pick up a new language or cook a new recipe.

▶ **Plan to be spontaneous:** Change up your regular routine. If you take an evening walk, occasionally venture along a new route. Once in a while alter the order of your day. Change the context or your environment and you'll feel your mind shift.

Unit 16: Viewing change as opportunity

Introduction

Many people view change as something to be feared, problematic and unknown, and yet a characteristic of resilient people is instead to see change as a potential opportunity for growth and development. Learning to accept change, even embrace it, is therefore a crucial skill in becoming more resilient. However, accepting change doesn't mean tolerating the unacceptable or allowing yourself to be taken advantage of – there will always be certain changes that you will want to resist and when this is the case it's important to voice your feelings, needs and values. It does mean, though, that you will be more open to many changes, and when there are changes that you cannot control, you learn to not to fear them and to view them as opportunities.

If we react to changes by wishing things were different, thinking negative thoughts, worrying, controlling, manipulating and becoming angry, these negative mindsets can cause anxiety, fear and fatigue. Instead of trying to control our circumstances, our circumstances can end up controlling us. If you're seeking to become more resilient, viewing change as opportunity can only enhance your life.

Depending on the size of the group you are coaching, this unit will take about 2 hours 30 minutes to complete.

Aims

This unit aims to teach learners about viewing change as opportunity. By the end of the session, they should be able to understand the different phases of change.

Activities

Opportunity for change

 1-2-1

Time: 30 minutes

Resources:

 Handout 16.1: Coping with change

 PowerPoint Slide 52: Approaches to change

PowerPoint Slide 53: Coping with change

Instructions:

Introduce the subject of viewing change as opportunity using the introduction to the unit before showing **PowerPoint Slide 52** and explaining that it can be helpful to think of change in terms of 'growing', 'evolving' or 'transforming'. This can help start making the shift in mind-set towards seeing change as an opportunity.

Ask the group if anyone can think of a time when they were dreading an upcoming change, but it turned out to be really positive. You may want to have an example of your own ready in case none of the learners have one.

Next, give out copies of **Handout 16.1: Coping with change** and show **PowerPoint Slide 53: Coping with change**. Ask the learners to consider the different techniques and to discuss them in pairs, each highlighting one in particular they will work on developing in themselves.

Finally, gather everyone back into the larger group to discuss, using the points below if needed.

 Discussion points: What was it like doing the activity? Which point are they each going to be working on and how?

Phases of change

 1-2-1

Time: 30 minutes

Resources:

 Handout 16.2: Phases of change

 PowerPoint Slide 54: Phases of change

Instructions:

Show **PowerPoint Slide 54: Phases of change** and give out copies of **Handout 16.2: Phases of change**.

Explain that there are six phases of change:

▶ Stage 1: Shock and denial, where the individual is in disbelief or paralysis.

▶ Stage 2: Searching, where the individual is uncertain of what to expect as a result of change and may feel either overwhelmed by potential negatives or impatient to move on.

▶ Stage 3: Confrontation, where the individual is beginning to realise the reality of change and may react with excitement or fear.

▶ Stage 4: Realisation, where the individual is starting accept that change is inevitable.

▶ Stage 5: Depression, where the individual realises that a loss needs to occur as the change opens up. Intellectual realisation is occurring possibly with emotional distress.

▶ Stage 6: Acceptance, where the individual has begun to emotionally accept the change with a sense of forward proactivity.

Hold a discussion on the subject of change using the handout.

Change your seat

 1-2-1

Time: 15 minutes

Instructions:

As the learners to leave the room and change the layout so that they'll have to randomly change where they are sitting. This way they can experience the emotions and feelings often associated with change. After the group gets sat back down and comfortable, start a discussion using some of the discussion points below.

At some point during this discussion, ask the learners to change seats once more.

 Discussion points: How did it feel to be asked to change seats? Did you view changing seats as an opportunity to sit with someone new or as an uncomfortable or undesirable change? What are some things that make people resistant to change?

If learners move back to their old seating arrangements after the exercise is over, ask them why it's difficult to maintain changes once they are made.

Encourage learners to consider and share their own personal emotions related to making changes. This is what makes the exercise powerful. Another twist to this activity might be to ask learners to change seats frequently, which also can help them enhance their personal ability to deal with change.

Change your look

Time: 20 minutes

Instructions:

Tell the learners that they're going to assist in an experiment about making changes.

Put the group into pairs and have each pair stand facing each other. Ask the learners to determine which one will observe and which one will make the changes. Tell the observer to study their partner closely because their partner will be making a few changes. Next, the observer from each pair should close their eyes and ask the other person to make five changes to their physical appearance. This could mean moving their watch from one wrist to the other, removing a shoe, taking off jewellery or a tie, or removing their glasses. Give them 30 seconds to complete the changes. The observer needs to identify as many changes as possible. Allow about 30 seconds for this.

Next, ask the partners to swap roles and try it the other way around.

Gather everyone back into a larger group and discuss the exercise using the points below if needed.

 Discussion points: How did it feel to be asked to make so many changes? What are some things that make people resistant to change? Why is it difficult to maintain changes once they are made?

Lifetime of change

 1-2-1

Time: 20 minutes

Resources: Handout 16.3: Lifetime of change

Instructions:

Give out copies of **Handout 16.3: Lifetime of change.**

Each set of pictures shows a progression from the past to the present day. For example, music players might show a gramophone through to an iPod, or writing methods might show the development from pen to typewriters to word processors.

Display these images around the room. Divide the group into smaller groups of differing ages and ask them to look at the images and discuss their experiences/ memories of these items. Use the discussion points below if needed.

Discussion points: What was it like to share experiences and memories? Each learner must have experienced change in different life areas. With hindsight, how have they managed these changes?

Ups and downs of change

 1-2-1

Time: 15 minutes

Resources:

 Handout 16.4: Ups and downs of change

Instructions:

Explain that the following exercise is important for understanding our gut reaction to change and starting to see change more positively.

For this activity, give each learner **Handout 16.4: Ups and downs of change** and ask them to write down beside each word if it makes them feel positive or negative.

Once everyone's had ten minutes or so to do that, hold a group discussion using the points below if needed.

 Discussion points: How did everyone feel about each word and why did they feel the way they did?

Lottery win

 1-2-1

Time: 30 minutes

Instructions:

Give a pen and sheet of paper to each learner. Explain that in this scenario you've just won the lottery and would like the learners to design a house for you. Give them a few minutes to start drawing, but then at some point before the pictures are done say you have changed your mind and you want them to design a boat. Again, at some point before they finish say you've changed your mind again and ask them to draw you a castle. Keep changing your mind until people get a bit fed up.

Hold a discussion on the exercise, using the point below if needed.

 Discussion points: As you changed your mind, did the learners notice some of the negative behaviours associated with change emerging, either in themselves or in others.

Write change

 1-2-1

Time: 10 minutes

Instructions:

Ask the learners to sign their name 10 times on a piece of paper. Ask them to do it again. Then ask them to put the pen in their other hand and write 10 signatures again. Next, ask them to do it again but distract them by talking throughout to take their mind of the exercise. At this point, most people will switch back to using their normal hands. Let them do this but after the exercise ask them why they switched back when you didn't tell them to. As far as you were concerned, the pen should have been in the other hand and you didn't say otherwise.

Hold a discussion about the exercise, using the points below if needed

 Discussion points: People will nearly always revert to what they know unless there's a conscious effort not to.

Journal reflections and post-session practice

Learners could reflect upon:

▶ A change-related situation in their past and how they dealt with it (with comments on any differences in how they might deal with it now).

▶ A current or immediate situation requiring change and how they might approach it.

Unit 17: Increasing pro-activity

Introduction

A pro-active approach to life focuses on eliminating problems before they have a chance to appear, which requires a high degree of foresight. A reactive approach is based on responding to events after they have happened, which often results in an inappropriate knee-jerk reaction. A resilient person sees ahead, when possible, and pro-actively plans for change.

Depending on the size of the group, this unit should take about 1 hour 45 minutes to complete.

Aims

This unit aims to teach learners about increasing pro-activity. By the end of the session, they should be able to:

▶ understand how active or reactive they are

▶ understand ways to over come procrastination

▶ see the link between creativity and proactivity.

Activities

Active or reactive?

 1-2-1

Time: 15 minutes

Resources:

 Handout 17.1: Increasing pro-activity

PowerPoint Slide 55: Reactive vs. proactive

PowerPoint Slide 56: Pillars of procrastination

Instructions:

Give out copies of the Handout 17.1 and introduce the subject of being reactive or pro-active. Open a discussion on the meaning of both terms before showing **PowerPoint Slide 55: Reactive vs. proactive**. The discussion could move onto the pros and cons of both states. Learners can share whether they think they are pro-active or reactive.

Next, introduce the idea of the four pillars of procrastination using **PowerPoint Slide 56: Pillars of procrastination:**

▶ **Low task value:** Tasks that we perceive as low value in terms of rewards. When a task is unpleasant or boring, we could attempt to tie more enjoyable activities to the task e.g. complete this project at the coffee shop. **Discussion points:** What kind of rewards have the learners used in the past? How have rewards changed their procrastination habits?

▶ **Personality:** Personality plays a role in procrastination. The upside is that although it's hard to control our personality, it is easier to control our environment. For instance if you love chocolate cake, it might be best to buy it frozen and keep it in the freezer than buy something fresh that is instantly accessible. **Discussion points:** What personality traits do the learners have that have contributed to overcoming procrastination or encouraged it?

▶ **Expectations:** If you expect to complete a task easily then you are less likely to procrastinate. It is usually the case that an impending task will be far less difficult than we imagine it to be, so if we can commit five-minutes to trying it out, we can see what it's really like. **Discussion points:** Ask learners to give examples of how expectations of a task has influenced their behaviour.

▶ **Goal failure:** Fear of failure is a real thing for many procrastinators. This pillar really has to do with being confident in your abilities. **Discussion points:** How has confidence in task completion influenced the learner's ability to engage with the job in hand?

Ways to overcome procrastination

 1-2-1

Time: 30 minutes

Resources:

 Handout 17.2: Overcoming procrastination

PowerPoint Slide 57: Overcoming procrastination

PowerPoint Slide 58: No more procrastination

Instructions:

Overcoming procrastination, which presents as a lack of motivation, involves examining your faulty thinking and related underlying fear, and assessing whether that fear is realistic. You can reframe faulty thinking by shifting the focus from the outcome to the process, which means greater self-awareness as the procrastination process occurs. As your cognitive awareness increases and is reframed, procrastination will reduce and achievement can occur, which will reinforce the positive.

Using **Handout 17.2: Overcoming procrastination**, open a discussion on common fears behind procrastination:

▶ **Fear of success:** By succeeding in a goal, you may feel that you are obligated to continue succeeding in the future. It may seem easier to put it off in order to avoid the additional burdens you associate with success.

▶ **Fear of impacting relationships:** Another of the causes of procrastination is a fear of how your success will affect relationships with others. If you succeed in implementing self-care strategies for a health issue, for example, will that strain the relationships with your partner who thrives on caring for you? It may seem easier to procrastinate to maintain the status quo with those around you. It might also be that you are trying to do something to please someone else.

▶ **Fear of rejection:** Putting yourself in front of others invites criticism. The uncertainty of how other people will react to you can stop you from taking action and is especially true if you don't have much confidence in yourself. Reframing rejection as feedback will help you improve your behaviour rather than taking it as a personal attack on you.

▶ **Fear of being imperfect:** Perfectionism is related to the fear of failure and that everything you do needs to be perfect otherwise you have failed. Perfectionism is setting yourself up with an impossible standard to meet so rather than experiencing a failure to meet an unreasonable expectation, you put off taking any action.

▶ **Fear of failure:** Because you are unsure of succeeding in your action, you put it off in order to avoid potential failure. If you never do it, there's no way to fail, but not taking action ensures a failure because you don't accomplish anything.

Ask the learners to work in small groups to discuss which of these fears might apply to them.

Using **PowerPoint slide 56: Overcoming procrastination** and **PowerPoint slide 57: No more procrastination** ask the learners to identify three approaches they might use and why.

Likes and loves

 1-2-1

Time: 30 minutes

Resources:

 Handout 17.3: Likes and loves

Instructions:

Explain to the group that their relationship to the activities in their lives can be a major factor in their level of procrastination. Give out copies of **Handout 17.3: Likes and loves** and ask them to think of all the activities they do in a typical week.

When they have completed their table, ask them to look at the amount of time they spend on the things they **need** to do and the things they **should** do. The more time allocated in these areas, the more stressed they will feel and the more likely they are to procrastinate.

Explain that the greater percentage of their time spent on their **likes** and **loves**, the more energised and productive they will be.

Explain that it isn't possible to eliminate all **needs** and **musts** but they think about how they can reduce, say by 10%, their **needs** and **musts**, and increase by 10% percent their **likes** and **loves**.

At the least, they should try to shift one hour per week from **needs** and **musts** to activities in the **likes** and **loves** categories.

Next, ask them to fill out Column C, indicating the changes they plan to make.

 Discussion points: What was it like doing the activity? What did they discover about themselves?

Stones

 1-2-1

Time: 30 minutes

Instructions:

Creativity is crucial for problem-solving and initiative. Ask the group to take a break outside in the fresh air for five minutes. While they are outside, ask them to find a small stone and think of a story or meaning for it – as zany or simple as they wish. When everyone is back in the room, ask them to share their stories about their stones to the group, each taking no longer than a few minutes.

 Discussion points: Discuss how this activity is different to typical work tasks e.g. it's creative – you are making something completely new and being 100% pro-active, rather than processing something and being mostly reactive, as in typical work tasks.

Creativity is extremely valuable in problem-solving and using personal initiative.

Journal reflections and post-session practice

Ask learners to reflect on how they relate to being pro-active in their life and keep a record of pro-active things they do throughout the week.

Unit 18: Personal networking

Introduction

As part of someone's personal network, you are showing yourself to be a caring person who is committed to maintaining relationships with others in order to support a given set of activities. Having a strong personal network requires being connected to a network of resources for mutual personal or professional development and growth. This pro-active stance increases resilience in times of change and challenge.

Depending on the size of the group you're working with, this unit will take about 2 hours 40 minutes to complete.

Aims

This unit aims to teach learners about personal networking. By the end of the session they should be able to identify and use ways to improve their networking skills.

Activities

Improving your social networks

 1-2-1

Time: 30 minutes

Resources:

 Handout 18.1: The benefits of a social network

Handout 18.2: Improving your social networks

 PowerPoint Slide 59: Benefits of a social network

PowerPoint Slide 60: Expanding your social network

PowerPoint Slide 61: Nurturing your social network

PowerPoint Slide 62: Help others to help you

Instructions:

Give out copies of **Handout 18.1: The benefits of a social network**, show **PowerPoint Slide 59** and explain that there are a number of benefits to having a solid personal support network:

▶ It can give you a sense of belonging. Spending time with people helps ward off loneliness and improves resilience.

▶ It can increase your sense of self-worth. Networking reinforces the idea that you're a good person to be around.

▶ It can improve your feeling of security. A social network can give access to information, advice, guidance and other types of assistance should they be needed.

Next, give out **Handout 18.2: Improving your social networks** and show **PowerPoint Slide 60**. Explain that the slide shows a list of techniques and steps the learners might take towards increasing the size of their social networks. Go through the list and then show **PowerPoint Slide 61**. Explain that nurturing an existing social network is also important or you might find that, when you need support the most, your friends are thin on the ground. Take them through the points on the PowerPoint slide, fielding any questions that might arise.

Show **PowerPoint Slide 62** and explain that it's really important not to shut yourself off from the support around you, and that some people make it very hard for others to be supportive. Using the slide, show the different ways in which the learners can make it easier for another to support them.

Next, ask the group to get into threes to discuss what they need personally from their networks and how they might improve them using what you have discussed as a guide.

After 10 minutes or so, get everyone back into a larger group to discuss their conclusions. Use the discussion points below if needed.

 Discussion point: What types of networks do learners need and why? How might they find appropriate networks?

Pair share

Time: 10 minutes

Instructions:

This activity will only work if the people in your group don't know each other very well, otherwise move onto the next activity.

If it is possible, pair the learners off with someone they don't know very well. Each pair has to find out three things they have in common but which are not obvious. Allow five minutes, and then come back into the group to discuss and share their findings.

Who am I?

Time: 15 minutes

Instructions:

Tape a piece of paper to each learner's back with the name of someone famous. That person then has to work out who they are using questioning and listening skills, but they can only ask closed questions that can be answered 'yes' or 'no'.

Get everyone back into the larger group to discuss the exercise.

 Discussion point: What was it like thinking of and asking questions based on only a yes or a no response? What was it like responding to a question where you could only answer yes or a no?

People hunt

Time: 15 minutes

Instructions:

Create a set of cards, each with one of the following sentences on:

▶ Find someone who lives the closest to you.

▶ Find someone who has been to the Tower of London.

▶ Find someone who likes Madeira cake.

▶ Find someone who has been on the radio.

▶ Find someone who loves roses.

▶ Find someone who has worked for a bank.

▶ Find someone who has run a marathon or half-marathon.

▶ Find someone who ridden a horse.

▶ Find someone who likes Wham!

▶ Find someone who has seen the film Dumbo.

▶ Find someone who has a cat.

Each learner is given a card and has to find a person who fits the bill, and fills in their name and contact information as they chat. This information can then be recorded and duplicated for all.

Get everyone back into the larger group to discuss the exercise.

 Discussion point: What was it like asking questions? What was it like being asked questions? What was it like revealing personal information?

Completed thought

Time: 15 minutes

Resources:

 PowerPoint Slide 63: Personal networking

Instructions:

This activity helps the learner to take ownership of their thoughts and feelings and to share them with others.

Show **PowerPoint Slide 63: Personal networking** and read the list of incomplete statements to the learners:

▶ Today I wish I were…

▶ The main reason I am here is…

▶ I choose friends who are…

▶ I think my best quality is…

▶ Today I am planning to learn…

▶ A pet peeve of mine is…

▶ Training sessions like this are usually…

▶ If I could change the world I would…

Hand out pens and paper and give the learners some time to write down the statements and then finish the thoughts in their own words. When they have finished, re-read each incomplete statement to the group and ask learners answer. Answers can be commented on and discussed.

Hold a discussion on the exercise, using the points below if needed.

 Discussion point: What is it like sharing information about yourself with people you don't know well? What is it like having others share information with you?

Flipchart sheets

 1-2-1

Time: 15 minutes

Instructions:

Give each learner two sheets of paper (ideally flipchart paper or A3) and several strips of masking tape.

▶ Ask everyone to write their first name and 'What I know about myself' at the top of one sheet. Give everyone 10 minutes to write relevant words or phrases on the sheet .

▶ On the other sheet, ask the learners to write 'What I want to know about you' and to list two things they would like to know about other people e.g. 'Do you live locally?' and 'Do you have any pets?'

▶ When everyone's finished, ask them stick up the sheets on the wall and mill around the room reading one another's sheets and writing relevant words or phrases on the 'What I want to know about you' sheet.

Get everyone back together to discuss the exercise, using the points below if needed.

 Discussion point: What was the activity like to do? What has come out of it?

Life events

 1-2-1

Time: 30 minutes

Resources:

 Handout 18.3: Life events

Instructions:

Give everyone a copy of **Handout 18.3: Life events**. Ask them to label the boxes with four life stages or characteristics. For example:

▶ 'Childhood', 'adolescence', 'adulthood', 'older age'

▶ '10 years ago', '5 years ago', 'now', 'in the future'

▶ 'My work life', 'my home life', 'my social life', 'my hobby time'

When they have done this, ask the learners to fill in each box by writing words or phrases, or draw pictures, that symbolise each box. Learners can work in small groups if they like, to share ideas.

Gather everyone back into one group to discuss the exercise, using the points below if needed.

 Discussion point: What was the activity like to do? What has come out of the activity?

Interviews

 1-2-1

Time: 30 minutes

Instructions:

Ask the group to get into pairs and ask them to pick a partner that they know the least about. Ask them to interview each other for about 10 minutes each way. You can prepare questions ahead of time or provide general guidelines for the interview. They need to learn about what each other likes about their jobs, their past jobs, about their family life and hobbies etc. After the interviews, reassemble the group and have each pair introduce their partner to the group.

Hold a discussion about the exercise, using the points below if needed.

 Discussion point: How was it to be the interviewer? How did you experience being interviewed?

Journal reflections and post-session practice

Ask the learners to reflect on what they:

▶ would like to gain from personal and professional networks and to identify appropriate support networks.

▶ have to offer others in terms of personal and professional support and how they might do this.

Unit 19: Increasing optimism

Introduction

The Oxford English Dictionary defines 'optimism' as: 'A tendency to take a hopeful view of things, or to expect that results will be good'. It could therefore be understood as reacting to problems with a sense of confidence and faith in one's abilities. Specifically, optimistic people believe that negative events are temporary and manageable, which makes them more resilient.

Depending on the size of the group you are coaching, this unit should take about 1 hour to complete.

Aims

This unit aims to teach learners about increasing their sense of optimism. By the end of the session, they should be able to think more positively.

Activities

Increasing optimism

 1-2-1

Time: 30 minutes

Resources:

 Handout 19.1: Optimism

 PowerPoint Slide 64: Increasing optimism

Instructions:

Show **PowerPoint Slide 64: Increasing optimism** and give out copies of **Handout 19.1: Optimism**. Ask the learners to go through the list on the handout and tick all of the boxes they think already apply to them. Of the boxes they left unticked, ask them to identify one area they could improve upon.

Next, ask them to get into pairs or groups of three to discuss the list for 10 minutes. Finally, get everyone back into a group and hold a general discussion, using the points below if needed.

 Discussion point: Which area did they each choose? What might they do to improve their optimism?

Gratitude journal

 1-2-1

Time: 15 minutes

Instructions:

The goal of this activity is to increase gratitude by keeping a daily journal. To get their journal started, ask the learners to complete their first entry (beginning with yesterday) where they might reflect on things, situations and people they are grateful for.

Although being grateful can result in positive effects, it is important to make sure that learners don't use gratitude as a way to avoid or deny the negative things in life such as being able to talk through a problem with someone. In addition, make sure they understand that gratitude is not only about big things. Drinking a cup a coffee, having a nice conversation, etc. are all good examples of things that one can be grateful for. Stress to the learners that gratitude is also not about downward comparison – you can be grateful for something without making a comparison with people who are worse off.

 Discussion point: What was it like to complete the activity?

The silver lining game

 1-2-1

Time: 20 minutes

Instructions:

Explain that you're going to play a game that involves finding the silver lining in difficult situations. Ask everyone to get into pairs and one member is going to bring up a negative event, ideally one that they have experienced personally, such as, 'I've just lost my job and I'm trying not to panic…' Their partner then offers a more positive approach to the problem, such as, 'Now that I've lost my job I'll have more time to…'. The first person then completes the sentence with a positive word or phrase. In this example they might say, '…to start the novel I've always wanted to write'.

After the pairs have switched roles a few times, gather everyone back into one group and discuss the exercise.

Journal reflections and post-session practice

To complete a daily gratitude journal, either a personal or professional one.

Unit 20: Increasing empathy

Introduction

Empathy differs from sympathy. Sympathy is an agreement of feeling with another, while empathy is more about understanding and sharing those feelings. Empathy is a deeper experience. To be empathic is not to lose one's self in shared experience, but to sense from within the other being's frame of reference while still maintaining a strong sense of self and resilience.

Depending on the size of the group, this unit should take about 30 minutes to complete.

Aims

This unit aims to teach learners how to increase their sense of empathy. By the end of the session, they should be able to identify what empathy is and clarify the benefits of using empathy.

Activities

Empathic skills

 1-2-1

Time: 30 minutes

Resources:

 Handout 20.1: Building empathetic skills

 PowerPoint Slide 65: Empathy

PowerPoint Slide 66: Benefits of empathy

Instructions:

Show **PowerPoint Slide 65: Empathy** and explain that the term 'empathy' describes the ability to sense other people's emotions, coupled with the ability to imagine what someone else might be thinking or feeling. Explain that researchers often differentiate between affective empathy and cognitive empathy. Use the PowerPoint slide to explain the difference between these.

Next, show **PowerPoint Slide 66: Benefits of empathy** and go through the list of benefits that increasing your empathetic skills will bring.

Give out copies of **Handout 20.1: Building empathetic skills** and, similarly, take the learner's through the list, encouraging discussion and giving them an opportunity to ask questions.

Journal reflections and post-session practice

Learners should observe themselves in action and note when they show empathy and how others react.

Unit 21: Laughter and humour

Introduction

Laughter and humour can help improve someone's resilience by easing tension, both with themselves and with others. While humour can sometimes be seen as a defence mechanism, it can also be a survival behaviour. Humour can be a diffuser. It can relax us enough to partially dissolve anxiety. It can bring people together in a shared experience.

Aims

This unit aims to teach learners about laughter and humour in relation to resilience. By the end of the session they should be able to identify and experience the benefits of laughter.

Activities

Laughter and humour

 1-2-1

Time: 30 minutes

Resources:

 Handout 21.1: Health benefits of laughter

Instructions:

Give out copies of **Handout 21.1: Health benefits of laughter** and explain that, according to some studies, laughter may provide a range of physical benefits. Talk the learners through the list of these potential benefits on the handout, encouraging discussion and answering any questions.

You could enhance this activity by asking people to tell their favourite joke or anecdote.

Discussion point: How does one define humour? What influences our sense of humour? How do cultural expectations influence humour?

Journal reflections and post-session practice

Watch a favourite comedy show or film. Notice what makes you laugh and why, and record your thoughts in your journal.

Unit 22: Extending purpose and meaning

Introduction

One of the most liberating things you can do in life is finding your purpose. This will give you all the meaning you require for your life. Your purpose is what wakes you up in the morning, what drives you, and what gives you energy and resilience.

Depending on the size of your group, this unit should take about 4 hrs, 30 minutes to complete.

Aims

This unit aims to teach learners about extending purpose and meaning. By the end of the session, they should be able to:

▶ understand the importance of finding meaning in life

▶ stay pro-active in exploring life meaning

▶ realise the importance of motivation in life purpose.

Activities

Embracing meaning

 1-2-1

Time: 30 minutes

Resources:

 Handout 22.1: Life areas

Instructions

Give out copies of **Handout 22.1: Life satisfaction** and ask the learners to rate how important various areas of their lives are on a scale of 1 to 4, where 1 is very important and 4 is not important at all.

Next, ask them to reorder the list into order from most important to least. For the four most important areas, ask the learners to write one or two sentences about how they would like to behave (not think or feel) in that area of their life. For example, 'I would like to be a kind, supportive and caring partner. I would also like to act as if I am worthwhile in relationships by asking for the things I need.'

Get everyone back into a larger group to discuss the exercise, using the points below if needed.

 Discussion point: How did you experience the activity? What was particularly challenging?

Write

 1-2-1

Time: 45 minutes

Instructions:

Ask the learners to write at the top of a sheet of paper '*What is my life purpose?*' and then ask them to free-associate and write whatever comes to mind, however mundane or far-fetched. For example, they might write, '*I have no idea,*' or, '*I want to be an astronaut*'. Whenever they write something that evokes an emotion for them, ask the learners to circle it. After about 15 minutes learners will start to run out of ideas.

Ask them to keep writing however, and encourage them to keep going however mundane. After about 30 minutes learners will find a theme emerging. For example, a theme about helping others may begin to emerge – 'I want to teach others', 'I want to help my children to be independent and compassionate' – or about taking control, or making changes. Whatever that theme is, the next step is to reflect on what has been written, see how it fits, and how the theme might be integrated into their life.

Finally, get everyone back into a larger group and discuss the activity, using the points below if needed.

 Discussion point: How did you experience the activity? What was particularly challenging?

Childhood dreams

 1-2-1

Time: 30 minutes

Instructions:

Ask the learners to remember childhood fantasies they had about their adult selves. These dreams tap into our core selves, before the practical necessities of earning a living, mortgages and growing up kicked in.

Ask the learners to think back to what they wanted to be when they grew up – fireman, doctor, princess, writer, whatever it may have been. Have any of these dreams persisted? If the dreams have changed over time (doctor to writer to ballet dancer) is there some unifying quality that runs through them? Helping others? Being creative or adventurous? Bringing joy or challenge?

When they have their theme in mind, e.g. helping others, ask them how might this translate into their daily life such as community work or their career.

Finally, get everyone back into a larger group and discuss the activity, using the points below if needed.

 Discussion point: How did you experience the activity? What was particularly challenging?

Being pro-active

 1-2-1

Time: 30 minutes

Instructions:

Being pro-active is about consciously shaping your time rather than passively taking what you can get.

Ask the learners to write 500 words about a great day they can remember and what made it special. Ask them to write about how it brought out the best in them and how that day relates to who they are now. Share in smaller groups or the larger group.

Hold a discussion on these issues using the points below if needed.

 Discussion point: How did you experience the activity? What was particularly challenging?

19 questions

 1-2-1

Time: 1 hour

Resources:

 Handout 22.2: Questions

Instructions:

Give everyone a copy of **Handout 22.2: Questions** and a few sheets of paper. Introduce the 19 questions and ask the learners to complete them as fully as they can on their own, in pairs or small groups. If they require more time they can do this as part of their post-session practise.

When everyone has had about 45 minutes to answer the questions, get everyone back into a large group and discuss the exercise, using the points below if needed.

 Discussion point: How did you experience the activity? What was particularly challenging?

Wheel of life

 1-2-1

Time: 15 minutes

Resources:

 Handout 22.3: Wheel of Life

Give out copies of **Handout 22.3: Wheel of Life**. To complete the wheel, learner's need to consider each of the life areas around the outer edge of the wheel and rate their level of satisfaction from 1 to 10, with 1 being not satisfied at all and 10 being very satisfied

 Discussion point: How did you experience the activity? What was particularly challenging?

Who you want to be (quick version)

 1-2-1

Time: 30 minutes

Instructions:

Ask the learners to write down continuously for five minutes everything that they want to be, do or have in their life. Ask them not to judge or censor what they put down. This is dreamtime!

Next, ask them to rate each of the things they have written down on a scale of 0-10 in terms of how much each one will help them live the kind of life they really want. A 0-rating indicates that achieving this goal would do absolutely nothing to help them get where they want to go. A 10-rating indicates that this goal is 100% taking them in the direction they want to go in.

Before they start, explain that many people find that when they rate things a clear pattern emerges. All the things they want to have or do rate very low on the scale whereas everything they want to be (e.g. happier, more at peace, less critical, a better parent etc.) tend to score much more highly. If you look after the 'be's', the 'do's' and 'have's' will follow.

Ask the learners to pick the top six of the things they wrote down and write why they are important to them. Then ask them to compare these to their Wheel of Life and give one tick for each segment which would improve from each 'being, doing or having'.

As a larger group, hold a discussion about the exercise using the points below if needed.

 Discussion point: How did you experience the activity? What was particularly challenging?

Motivation

 1-2-1

Time: 30 minutes

Resources:

Handout 22.4: Motivation

Handout 22.5: Understanding motivation

Instructions:

Motivation is the psychological force that initiates, guides and maintains goal-oriented behaviours. It is what causes you to take action. These inner conditions such as wishes, desires and goals activate us to move in a particular direction. The strongest motivators are: achieving results, being valued and made to feel important, being included and accepted by an admired group, competing, gaining influence and status and earning more money.

Using **Handout 22.4: Motivation**, open a group discussion on ways motivation can help you find meaning in your life.

Next, clarify the different types of motivation:

Intrinsic or internal motivation – Intrinsic motivation refers to motivation that is driven by an enjoyment in the task itself. When you are intrinsically motivated, you are more likely to engage in the task willingly as well working to improve yourself. '*Intrinsic motivation occurs when we act without any obvious external rewards. We simply enjoy an activity or see it as an opportunity to explore, learn, and actualise our potentials.*' (Coon & Mitterer, 2010). You are likely to be intrinsically motivated if you:

▶ attribute good results to factors under your own control

▶ are interested in mastering a topic or skill

▶ believe you have the skills to be effective agents in reaching your desired goals.

Ask learners what increases intrinsic motivation for them before introducing **Handout 22.5: Understanding motivation** and exploring the following list.

▶ Challenge: You are likely to be more motivated when you pursue goals that have personal meaning, relate to your self-esteem, when performance feedback is available, and when attaining the goal is possible.

▶ Curiosity: Internal motivation is increased when something about the activity stimulates you to want to learn more.

▶ Control: We want control over ourselves and our environment and want to determine what we pursue.

▶ Co-operation and competition: Intrinsic motivation can be increased in situations where you gain satisfaction from helping others and in cases where you are able to compare your own performance favourably to that of others.

▶ Recognition: We enjoy having our accomplishments recognised by others, which can increase internal motivation.

Extrinsic or external motivation – Extrinsic motivation refers to the performance of an activity in order to attain an outcome, whether or not that activity is also intrinsically motivated. Extrinsic motivation comes from outside of you e.g. money for showing the desired behaviour or the threat of punishment. Competition is in an extrinsic motivator because it encourages the performer to win and to beat others, not simply to enjoy the intrinsic rewards of the activity.

 Discussion point: How did you experience the activity? What was particularly challenging?

Journal reflections and post-session practice

Who you want to be (long version)

Stage one

First, write down the person you want to be – the characteristics that you want to have, the things you want to own and the things you want to do. Let your imagination run wild. Once your list is written, allow your mind to reflect on it over the next few days.

Stage two

Second, start reducing the items on your list. This process will eventually give you a list (no longer than half a sheet of A4) of the things that are most important to you and that are in alignment with your core values and beliefs. For each item on the list, ask yourself the following questions:

▶ Why do I want this?

▶ Why do I want to own this?

▶ Why do I want to be this kind of person?

Write each answer in one positive sentence, for example, 'I want this because…' As you go through the list, cross out anything if you can't answer any of these questions. Don't erase it completely, however, because you may be able to answer it later.

You now should have narrowed down your list even further. Write a new list with just those items still left on it. You will should now have a list of goals that you want to achieve and you know why.

Stage three

Look at the list of goals you created in stage two and see how they match up to the areas in your Wheel of Life. For example, depending on the areas in your Wheel of Life, you might ask yourself, if I get this thing, if I become this person, will I be happier? Is it going to improve my health? Is it going to improve my financial situation? Will being this person, having this, doing that etc. improve my environment? Will it give me better family relationships? Will it improve my social life? How is it going to impact upon my life?

Measure each goal against the areas of your Wheel of Life that you have deemed most important. Every time that you can answer, 'Yes, this goal will improve this area of my life', give it a mark. Ask yourself the questions in relation to all the areas of your wheel. Total up the marks for each goal. Which goals scored highly and which achieved a low score?

Stage four

Next you need to evaluate further. For each item on your list, consider whether taking steps to achieve that goal will take you closer to your overall objective.

Stage five

Next, look at your top 10 goals (or, if you have fewer than 10, do this for all your goals) and consider what kinds of goals they are. They should fall into on one of four types:

▶ **Ongoing goals.** These are goals you can work towards daily on an ongoing basis. For example, your goal may be to devote a certain number of hours per day to practising piano. Be specific about your goals. It is up to you to decide how you will achieve your goal on a daily basis.

▶ **Short-term goals.** These are goals that can be achieved within a week to a month. An example of a short-term goal might be to contact your old friends.

▶ **Medium-term goals.** These take between a month and a year to achieve, such as reaching your target weight.

▶ **Long-term goals.** These can take a year or more to complete but will have a definite end, unlike your ongoing goals – for example, a change in career.

All yours goals need to have a realistic time-scale for achievement. Now, identify your goals as ongoing, short, medium or long-term.

Stage six

For stage six, take each one of the sentences attached to your goals during stage two and elaborate in more detail why you want to reach the goal. Ninety percent of success in achieving you goals is all about the 'why', only 10% is the 'how'. People fail to achieve their goals because they have not fully explored the reasons why they want to do something, what it will mean for them and what the benefits will be. They have not become fully associated with and immersed in their goal.

Now you have created for yourself a list of reasons why you must have something, do something or become someone – a reason for each of the goals on your list. You have got to 'be' before you can 'do'. You have got to 'do' before you can 'have'. Now you know why you want these things, you can go on to the next stage.

Stage seven

In stage seven, take each of your top 10 goals (or fewer, depending on how many you have) and create a 'to do' list. This will never get finished because as soon as you take things off, more go back on. They are generally about activity. For each goal, get fully associated with the 'why' again and start to write down all of the actions that you would a) be prepared to take, and b) must take to achieve that goal. Don't start judging whether you will or will not at this stage. Just write everything down.

Stage eight

Next, make new lists of the following:

▶ The people you might need to get in touch with for help and advice.

▶ The people you need to work with.

The Resilience Coaching Toolkit © Pavilion Publishing and Media Ltd and its licensors 2017.

▶ The skills you might need to develop, what you might need to learn and what you need to improve your understanding of.

Do this for each individual goal.

Finally

When all eight stages are completed you'll have an almost complete picture of where you want to be and a reasonably complete list of goals. Close your eyes, wander out into the future and see yourself at whatever age this healthy, hard-working, happy, motivated person that you've become or want to become, is likely to be. Go back over your life and tell yourself what has and is still happening. Write down all the amazing things you did, became, things you managed to accumulate in your life that were important to you, the places you have been, the people you have touched and the changes you have made. Write it as though it has happened or is real right now. You have now designed an amazing life.

Wellbeing Professionals At Work

Laurel Alexander's book *"How to Incorporate Wellbeing Coaching into Your Therapeutic Practice"* (Jessica Kingsley) can be purchased from Amazon.

Wellness Professionals at Work is an established provider of learning opportunities, delivering recognised coaching qualifications and CPD courses to health and well-being professionals wanting to improve best practice. We offer flexible delivery, quality content and speed of completion with the choice of supervised skills development, face-to-face or online.

Two courses we offer which you may be interested in is the Diploma in Resilience Coaching and the Integrated Diploma in Resilience and Wellness Coaching.

We also offer the two-day CPD Train the Resilience Coach based on the *Resilience Coaching Toolkit* which carries CPD points from the CPD Certification Service and the National Council of Psychotherapists.

Our courses are accredited and recognised by:

Association for Coaching (AC)

Wellness Professionals at Work is an organisational and training provider member of the Association for Coaching (AC) and is committed to the ethical development of coaching as a profession.

National Council of Psychotherapists (NCP)

Wellness Professionals at Work is a training provider member of the NCP as well as being an accredited CPD centre.

Complementary Medical Association (CMA)

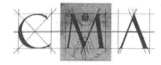

Wellness Professionals at Work is a recognised and authorised CPD course provider of the Complementary Medical Association (CMA).

By choosing us as your learning partner, you can be assured that the knowledge and skills gained from our courses are likely to be used throughout your working life. For more information:

Laurel Alexander
Founder of Wellness Professionals at Work and Director of Studies

W: www.wellnessprofessionalsatwork.com.

T: 01273 564030

E: info@laurelalexander.co.uk